United Indian Patriotic Association

Showing the seditious character of the Indian national congress and the opinions held by eminent natives of India who are opposed to the movement

United Indian Patriotic Association

Showing the seditious character of the Indian national congress and the opinions held by eminent natives of India who are opposed to the movement

ISBN/EAN: 9783337305628

Printed in Europe, USA, Canada, Australia, Japan

Cover: Foto ©Suzi / pixelio.de

More available books at **www.hansebooks.com**

Pamphlets issued by the United Indian Patriotic Association.

No. 2.

SHOWING

THE SEDITIOUS CHARACTER

OF

THE INDIAN NATIONAL CONGRESS

AND THE

OPINIONS HELD BY EMINENT NATIVES OF INDIA

Who are OPPOSED to the Movement,

~~~~~~~~~~~~~~~~

ALLAHABAD:

PRINTED AT THE PIONEER PRESS.

1888.

TABLE OF CONTENTS.

Government, a desire to commit suicide has never been included. To produce anyhow a sensation in England they have placarded the streets with notices, stating that their Debating Society represents the opinions of 200,000,000 people, the monstrous absurdity of which assertion can be only realised by people resident in India, though its falsity may be seen by a mere glance at the appendix of this pamphlet, in which it is shown that not only have large public meetings all over India condemned the movement, but more than forty political associations have expressed their bitter hostility to it. To the Englishman in England they appeal against the alleged tyranny of his brother in India. They profess to be the champions of a down-trodden nationality, ground down by a greedy band of Anglo-Indian officials. That they represent not a nation, but a party recruited from certain small classes in a certain group of Indian nations—(mostly nations down-trodden before English rule, but now raised by means of the colleges created by Anglo-Indians),—and that they are stoutly opposed by men in all parts of the continent belonging to other classes, and more especially the sturdier and more martial races, are facts which the United Indian Patriotic Association is anxious to bring prominently before the eyes of the English public. The selection of writings published in this pamphlet will, it is hoped, make this sufficiently clear.

The writers belong to the two main racial divisions of India, Hindus and Muhammadans. The

Raja of Bhinga is a Baron of Oudh, belonging to the chivalrous and brave caste of Rajputs, the second and most highly esteemed of the four castes of Manu, the fighting or ruling caste. This caste ruled India before the Muhammadan invasion, and during the Muhammadan empire held the highest positions of military command. The Raja's ancestors were men of high rank under the Muhammadan Emperors, and their deeds of prowess have been recorded by the Raja in a short monograph. The Rajputs of Oudh have entirely thrown in their influence against the Congress, and their most illustrious names will be found in the list of members of the United Indian Patriotic Association. The whole fighting force of the Hindus of Oudh is subject to their influence. A second Hindu name of great significance in this compilation is that of the Maharaja of Benares, a nobleman of the old school, and the representative of a famous royal house. Turning to the Muhammadan writers, Sir Syed Ahmed is the chief leader of the Muhammadans throughout India. Mr. Syed Hosain Bilgrami is a high official in the Nizam's Government, and is distinguished for his literary abilities. Munshi Imtiaz Ali is Legal Adviser of the political association of the Barons of Oudh, and is a man of great influence in that Province. Chaudhri Nasrat Ali is a taluqdar of Oudh. Mr. Muhammad Hosain Hakim practices at the Bombay Bar. But the most important name in the whole list of opponents of the National Congress is that of the first Patron of the Association, His Highness

the Nizam of Hyderabad. The premier Prince of
India, ruling a country as large as that of a first-
rate European power, his name is regarded with
affection and esteem by Muhammadans in all parts
of the continent. Sir W. W. Hunter seems to
think that the political forces represented by the
National Congress are so great that the British
Government, if it sought to thwart them, would
wreck itself in the attempt. Suffice it to say that
the name of the Nizam alone is by itself ten times a
match for them.

The members of the United Indian Patriotic
Association, while strongly opposed to the introduction of representative institutions as utterly
unfitted for the present state of the country, yield
to none in their desire for the true advancement
of the people. But they do not believe that the
way to secure this end is by an effort to wrest the
power from the hands of the Indian Government,
or by attempting to coerce it, either by uninformed
British electors, or by the ignorant masses of
India. While recognising the value of the strong
sense of justice towards India that animates
the public in England, they do not believe this
feeling to be so superficial in Englishmen as to
evaporate entirely on their arrival in India, nor
do they admit that Anglo-Indian statesmen have
shown a want of regard for the good government, progress, and advancement of the country.
They therefore invite the cultured English public to
hesitate before forming a judgment on the present

complicated political questions at issue in India, and if they have an hour to spare, to peruse the collection of speeches and articles published in this pamphlet.

THEODORE BECK,
Hony. Editor, United Indian Patriotic
Association.

DEMOCRACY NOT SUITED TO INDIA.

By the Raja of Bhinga.*

A VERY able pamphlet with the above title has appeared, analysing the constitution, aim, and pretensions of the *National Congress*, and discussing the fundamental principles of Indian politics. A few extracts are here given :—

In the Preface the Raja says :—" I entreat the martial races of India in general, and my Rajput brothers in particular, to pause before they decide to take any part in the aforesaid movement which, if not confined to Bengal and Madras, cannot fail to end in misrule and anarchy."

An examination of the proposals of the National Congress is thus summed up :—" They are for the most part crude, ill-considered and unpractical, showing no signs of political ability or insight, and affording no ground for anticipating political results of any value from the introduction of representative institutions into India."

As to the methods employed by the agitators, the writer says :—" The real, though not always the avowed, object is to persuade the people that the power of Government has in various ways been abused, and ought to be diminished, and that a large proportion, if not all the ills to which they are

---

* This pamphlet may be obtained at the *Pioneer* Press, Allahabad, India. Price,—annas 8 (8 pence).

subject, are the direct result of the action or the
negligence of Government. Consider first the effect
which an agitation, primarily directed to this end, is
likely to produce in India. It is true that the
speeches of the agitators abound in loyal protesta-
tions. It is a common practice at the Congress
meetings to propose cheers for the Queen-Empress,
to express the most exaggerated attachment to the
person of the Sovereign, and even occasionally to
acknowledge the benefits which India owes to the
British rule. But the whole thing is obviously
forced and artificial, designed to catch the ignorant
or unwary in England, and, it must be admitted,
with considerable apparent success. It is of small
practical advantage to express devotion to the
Queen-Empress when everything done by her servants is persistently denounced and misrepresented,
or to extol British administration in the past while
everything is done to weaken and discredit it in the
present or future. The British rule to which all
this loyalty is professed, is the rule of past time and
distant places ; the British rule as it is here and now
is held up on every side to reprobation ; and which
of the lessons is the more likely to be learnt by the
ignorant and unthinking masses ? The third Congress report begins with a glowing description of
the extraordinary results achieved by a century of
English rule. ‘British education and British literature instinct with the highest principles of civil and
religious liberty ; British history and the examples
of Britain's noblest sons—these the grandest gifts

ever bestowed by conquerors on a subject nation, poured with an unselfish hand into the minds of a noble, though fallen people, alone rendered this great Congress a possibility.' This is for English consumption. The ' Conversation between Maulvi Fariduddin and Ram Bakhsh,' which is being circulated among the masses, adopts a very different tone. There is no eloquence wasted about the Queen-Empress or ' the grandest gifts ever bestowed by conquerors on a subject nation.' The object of the pamphlet is to contrast India as it is under the British Government in its present form with India as it would be under representative institutions. It is in the form of a dialogue between a High Court pleader and a villager, to whom the former explains how all the evils which the peasantry suffer should be attributed to the form of Government now existing, and will disappear if it is reconstituted on a popular basis."

The effect of the spread of literature of this stamp is thus described in the Raja's pamphlet :—

"There can be no doubt that such writings constitute a most serious political danger. It is not as if they were addressed to people trained in the methods of European democracy and accustomed to distinguish between the most severe criticism of the measures of Government and the desire to destroy its authority. The readers of the ' Conversation between Maulvi Fariduddin and Ram Bakhsh' are wholly destitute of the experience which would make such a notion intelligible. The only idea that

denunciations of Government and assertions that it
is the cause of their poverty and all their other misfortunes can possibly convey to their minds is that
what is necessary is a general rebellion and the des-
truction of every European in the country.   This
feeling is enormously strengthened by the attitude
assumed by Government towards the agitators and
their preaching.   The ignorant masses are as little
able to understand toleration by Government of its
enemies as to understand that the enemies of
Government do not desire its overthrow.   Such
toleration is universally regarded as mere cowardice
and the consciousness of weakness."

We close our extracts from the pamphlet with
the following :—

" It is time to consider very shortly the question
recently so much discussed—' In what will it end ?'
The answer given by many whose opinions are entitled to respect is that, unless checked, it will end in
revolution and massacre.   They see that the agitators are lighting fire close to the most combustible
and explosive materials, that no hand is raised to
stop them, but that on the contrary well meaning
men of undoubted loyalty and patriotism are, with
extraordinary infatuation, encouraging them in their
work.   They see that every grievance is being fostered under the pretence of constitutional reform, that
in the name of national unity and the fusion of races
every form of internal dissension is stirred up, and
that in the name of peace and good-will between
England and India the people are being taught

to hate their rulers. It may well seem that to all this one end only is possible.

"But notwithstanding these considerations, it is too early to despair, and there is still abundant ground for hope. If the conclusions stated in the earlier chapters of this work are sound, the agitators do not yet represent the people of India or more than the smallest fraction of the people. Moreover, those whom they do represent can never themselves be dangerous except indirectly and by inciting others. The brave races of India are as yet untouched ; the natural leaders of the people still hold aloof from the work of destroying the results of the patient and devoted labours of a century. If a strong and fearless policy is adopted and consistently adhered to, there is nothing to fear from the designs of the agitators."

IN WHAT WILL IT END?

By Mr. Theodore Beck.

(FROM THE " PIONEER.")

Jack Cade: There shall be in England seven halfpenny loaves sold for a penny. All shall eat and drink on my score; and I will apparel them all in one livery, that they may agree like brothers and worship me their lord. Go to Sirrah! Tell the king from me that for his father's sake, Henry the Fifth, I am content he shall reign; but I'll be protector over him. Now show yourselves, men; 'tis for liberty. We will not have one lord, one gentleman. Away, burn all the records of the realm: my mouth shall be the Parliament of England.—(*Shakespeare: Henry VI, Part II, Act IV*).

I.

As it is my belief that the agitation of which the National Congress is the visible head will, if unchecked, sooner or later end in a mutiny, with its accompanying horrors and massacres, followed by a terrible retaliation on the part of the British Government, bringing absolute ruin for the Musalman, the Rajput and other brave races, and resulting in the retardation of all progress, I wish to place before my countrymen the reasons which have led me to form this opinion, and to invite a refutation of the arguments adduced. We had a sharp lesson in 1857 about the inadvisability of not studying the undercurrents of thought in India, and I fear that if we let the Bengali Press and the Congress agitation go on for another ten or twenty years, we shall have as disagreeable an awakening as we had then.

There are two things to be distinguished in the National Congress : *first*, its object ; *second*, its *modus operandi* or method.   In its method lies the danger. Were its object not visionary and unattainable, but wise and beneficial, the danger would still exist, unless a radical change were made in the means by which it was sought to effect the object.   But before pointing out the latent danger of the method, let me say a few words about the object—the proposed reconstitution of the Legislative Councils.

One of the speakers in the last Congress did me the honour of alluding to some criticisms of mine on the proposal to introduce parliamentary government into India.   He said, and many papers which criticised me also said, that the intention of the Congress stopped far short of a parliament, and was confined to the scheme about Legislative Councils, and therefore that all my arguments were beside the mark.   But I note in the "Tamil Catechism," printed at the end of the report of the Madras Congress, the following question and answer :—

"*Q.*—Then you think the Congress will really be of great use ?"

"*A.*—Yes, most certainly ; for one of the best means of promoting the welfare of India is the establishment of a Grand Council on the lines of the English Parliament, and if persevered in and wisely guided and supported by the whole country, the Congress will gradually, when India is fit for this, be converted into an Indian Parliament, which will take the place of the sham Councils of the present day."

From this and a hundred other indications, I conclude that I was right in thinking that a parliament is what the promoters of this movement have as their goal, and that the assurance that the only object is a reconstitution of the Legislative Councils is the language of diplomacy. But I will leave the parliament aside. I will suppose that the ultimate ambition of the Congresswallas is their proposed reform of the Legislative Councils, and that if Government suggested going a step further, every man who now supports the Congress would turn round and oppose such a proceeding as too radical. I will now discuss this measure, which its advocates complacently describe as extremely moderate.

The proposal, as formulated by the National Congress, contains seven distinct clauses, some of them embodying several distinct propositions, and to all these clauses and propositions six hundred men gave unanimous consent ! In the first clause it is stated that the number of members on the Legislative Councils is to be "materially increased," and of these not less than one-half are to be elected, while not more than one-fourth are to be members *ex-officio*, and not more than one-fourth nominated by Government. In the sixth clause it states that "all legislative measures and all financial questions, including all budgets, whether these involve new or enhanced taxation or not, are to be necessarily submitted to and dealt with by these Councils." It will thus be seen that the elected members have only to gain one supporter among the official or nominated members to secure a majority and be

absolute. The use to which this reformed Council is
to be put, is thus described by Mr. Surendranath
Banerji, the proposer of the motion:—" It is impossible to think of a domestic grievance, or a matter of
domestic complaint, which will not be remedied, if the
constitution of the Councils were changed and re-
modelled according to our programme. Talk of the
separation of judicial from executive functions, why,
the reform would be effected at once, if we had the
making of our own laws. Talk of the wider employment of our countrymen in the public service, why the
Queen's Proclamation would be vindicated to the
letter (applause), if we had some control over the
management of our domestic concerns. (Applause).
You fret and fume under the rigour of an income-tax
which touches even the means of subsistence, why
the incidence of the tax would be altered, the minimum raised, if we had anything to do with the imposi-
tion of the tax, or if we were permitted to modify it.
(Applause)." Some further notice of the magnitude of
the demand may be gathered from the philanthropic
froth of an English lawyer who is innocently trying
to ignite the gunpowder. "The day will come," said
Mr. Eardley Norton, " when an infinitely larger and
truer freedom will be yours, when the great question
of taxation will be within your grasp, when you will
in truth realise that you have got something more
than mere potential power, when you shall place
your hand upon the purse-strings of the country and
the Government. (Loud and continued applause).
Money is power, whether it be in the hands of an

individual or of a Government. He who has the
dispensing of money is he who has the control of all
ultimate authority. (Cheers). Once you control the
finances, you will taste the true meaning of power
and of freedom.   (Cheers)."

Now let us suppose these Councils constituted,
and let us suppose Government to propose a
measure, for example, the income-tax, to which these
high-minded democrats object.   There are two pos-
sibilities.   Either the elected members support the
Government, or they oppose it. It is pretty clear
which they will do ; but suppose, for the sake of argument, they support it.   Is anyone so foolish as to
imagine that it will be less unpopular because the
elected members agree to it ?   Everyone will think
that Government coerced them.   They cannot take
on their shoulders the odium and the responsibility
which everyone rightly attributes to Government.
Nor can Government shirk this responsibility.
Now, suppose they oppose the Government.   Is it
conceivable that under these circumstances Government could continue to govern ?   They want money
to pay the army and their servants, and the Council
refuses them.   They are to bear the weight of the
responsibility ; they are to protect the country
from Russia ; they are to prevent the martial races
of Upper India, Behar, and other places from throwing off the yoke of the native rulers belonging to
castes and races whom they despise, placed over
them by competitive examination ; and yet they
are to have no power.   The electorate is to " taste

the true meaning of power and of freedom "—without the responsibility. Well, in this case of Government finding itself frustrated by the Council—the case to which Mr. Surendranath Banerji looks forward with delight, the only case in fact which gives any point to the Congress proposal—what is Government to do? It must do one of two things : either abolish the Council, or retire from the country. The former case will cause great exasperation ; the latter we do not intend to do, nor do the Congresswallas want it. The experiment of these mixed Councils has been tried in the West Indies, and Mr. Froude points out that it is one of the causes of their decline in prosperity. The elected members, he says, always vote against Government, and thereby the greatest amount of friction is produced and the greatest unpopularity of the Governor. In Jamaica, when Government overrode the decision of the elected members, a Negro gentleman, named Gordon, a well-meaning agitator, called a big public meeting against Government. The Negroes went armed. Some English soldiers went to see : a fight ensued, the Negroes began to ravage the land, the country was put under martial law, Gordon was hanged, and the Constitution was abolished. That incident gives a graphic picture of what would probably take place in India, but on a hundred times bigger scale, if this proposal of the Congress were adopted.

But there is a minor measure which Government might adopt, without such disastrous consequences. A change might be made in the present Legislative Council by which a small number of native members might be elected by specified constituencies, no increased power being given to the Councils, and no handle in the executive. Such a reform would possess a specious resemblance to the proposal of the National Congress, and it is not inconceivable that Government might throw it out as a sop. I venture to say that this would, in my opinion, be a fatal mistake. It would as much satisfy their appetite as a sparrow would that of a hungry tiger, and it would give a gigantic stimulus to the whole movement. Moreover, when there are so few seats, it would be very unfair to give any constituencies or interests a permanent footing on the Council. The Parsees, for example, are a wealthy and important community. If they were represented according to their numbers in an Indian Parliament, then in a Parliament of the preposterous dimensions of 3,000 members there ought to be only one Parsee. The measure would be unfair on those who were left unrepresented. For the elected members would consider it their duty to push the interests of their constituencies. And thus the Government, too, would lose, for this duty towards the constituency would conflict with the Imperial duty which alone should animate the members. A further objection to this measure is, that it would insert the thin end of the wedge for the agitators ever to hammer at, and it would disguise the true nature of the British power in India, which is, and must be, a despotism, controlled not by ignorant masses, but by the law of duty. A cosmopolitan bureaucracy, with the ultimate authority in the hands of Englishmen, is, it seems to me, the only possible ambition for the Indian political idealist.

Besides this main demand of the National Congress, there are a number of minor proposals which are some objectionable, some unobjectionable. I do not propose to discuss them because they would carry me far away from the main thesis. They have to be noticed only as showing in a plain and unmistakable way one of the principles constituting the *modus operandi* of the agitators. The principle is this :—That the Congress seeks to strengthen its hold on the community by opening its doors to every kind of political grievance. Thus, while bent on one main object— to seize the reins of Government—it encourages everyone who cares for some other object to join and vote for the representative proposal, in the hope that the mighty uproar, when directed on his pet scheme, will give it a chance. The army was held out as a bait to the Mahomedans, but they caught sight of the hook. The unofficial Europeans and Eurasians with amazing simplicity have walked into the trap, and have of course been received with open arms. Anyone with a following and a grievance is welcome. It all adds fuel to the fire. I am now well launched off on the discussion of the method of the Congress, and I have to justify the proposition I made at the commencement of this

discussion.   And I ask now—What will be the effect
of this ?   What will be the result of keeping open a
great grievance-shop in this Empire ?   What will be
the effect on the minds of people who go and listen
for four or five days to glowing accounts of injustice and mismanagement, brought in from all parts
of the continent ; to the brutality of this damnable
political agent, who " betrays his trust to his conscience, his country, and his Queen;" to the cruelty
of the Government which causes "thousands of their
countrymen and countrywomen to be killed every
year by tigers and leopards " because of the Arms
Act?   And when you have carefully hunted out every
grievance—and I suppose no one has no complaint—
and have collected them and tabulated them, and
when the whole year round the press reeks with
them, and once a year all the grievance-mongers
come together and blow off their eloquence, will it
strengthen the Empire ?   It will be a great running
sore which will never heal because the ambition of
the agitator will demand fresh grievances as fast as
any are removed, and he will create them if they do
not exist.   There will be no difficulty in this.   In
every country there are men dying of starvation; there
are miscarriages of justice and acts of oppression—
this is the sad order of this world.   Who that has
once seen the East End of London, with its million
inhabitants sunk in squalor, dirt, and misery, their
faces ingrained with degradation and suffering, can
forget the terrible sight?   Or the spectacle of our
great civilised city at night, with the drunken men

reeling out of the public houses and the brazen faces of the women? There is nothing so shocking as this in India. But suppose London were under foreign rule instead of being under "the most enlightened Government in the world," all these miseries would be wrongly put down to the foreigner, and the forces of anarchy would arise in irresistible strength. So it will be in India. The agitators tell the people that all their ills, the miserable poverty of sections of them, are due to the English, and that their nostrum is a magic wand that will set all right. The manufacture of grievances is already in full swing. The Congress could no more get on without grievances than an English political party could without a programme. For without grievances it would die. And the Congress has to be kept alive because, if Mr. Hume's ambition is to be realised, it will some day wake up and find itself a real Parliament.

I have now to discuss the spirit in which these grievances are laid before the public, and the means adopted for stirring up the ignorant. I maintain that this spirit and these means are disloyal and seditious. I must now define the precise meaning that I attach to the term "disloyal." For I shall at once be told that the raising of three cheers for the Queen is a frequent phenomenon in Congress meetings, and that many of the delegates not only say but feel they would be sorry for the English to leave India. Granted. To doubt the fact would be to doubt their sanity. But I still call them disloyal. If a boy abused and injured his father to whom he owed his means of support, I should call him an undutiful son in spite of the fact that he knew that his father's death would be his own ruin. The loyalty which consists of not wishing the British army to go, and yet of doing everything to weaken the Government, trying to seize from it all the power of rule and undermining its influence in the hearts of the people, is a kind of loyalty I loathe. I had rather have an honest foe than an insidious and backbiting friend. Real loyalty tries to strengthen the Government and breathes a spirit of gratitude. The other loyalty is identical in its effects with the disloyalty of a wily enemy. We judge of men by their deeds and not by their words, and we judge of their loyalty by whether their actions tend to remove the soreness from the hearts of men or to aggravate it.

Coming now to the means adopted in this Congress agitation, the essential feature is that they do not confine their action to the educated classes, but make every effort to extend it to the ignorant. This tomfoolery about delegates necessitates it. Mass meetings are held and addressed by fiery orators ; and inflammatory literature is circulated in the vernacular. Only the man who believes in the infinite gullibility of the Englishman can dare state that the masses in India can understand the question of the reform of the Legislative Councils, of which they have never even heard the name. As easily could a company of English rustics comprehend the philosophy of Kant. To understand how

the Hindu is to govern India under the cloak of the
British name by means of a representative system
imported from England, the English with their
swords standing by as the willing slaves of their
rulers, is a conception sufficiently difficult to tax the
intellectual resources of even a Calcutta graduate.
One broad issue arises at once to the popular mind.
British rule or Native rule? And when the English
are abused and the grievances of the people are dwelt
on, can there be any doubt on which side they will
decide? To illustrate this by an example :—At a
certain town a meeting was held, and as usual they
secured as chairman (by what means I will not spe-
cify) a Mahomedan, so as to keep up the deceitful
farce that the Mahomedans are with them. He
was an uneducated nobleman, with nothing but the
primitive ideas of rule in his head prevalent in the
savage land from which he hails. They stood up
and abused the English before him, one man calling
English Assistant Collectors monkeys. What will
be the effect on the mind of that wild and ignorant
chief? I know of an unlettered Thakur Baron in a
Native State who asks of his friends when the next
mutiny is coming, being quite indifferent which side
he takes, but longing for something to relieve the
monotony of his dull life. I will not give his address
lest the Congresswallas should invite him to be
chairman of a meeting in his country, or should send
him a copy of the pamphlet to which I shall allude
further on, when I shall bring more specific charges
of disloyalty.

II.

In the first part of this discussion I pointed out that the very constitution of the National Congress was such that it was bound to foster a spirit of discontent and mutiny in the people ; that a Grievance Hall, as a permanent institution, would be like a running sore bringing all kinds of aches and pains to the body politic ; and that the delegate system, based as it was on popular support and popular discontent, was bound to encourage a kind of public speaking and literature, the object of which would be to picture in glowing colours the injustice of Government. And thus, however strong and however loyal the hands that controlled the movement, however much they might wish not to inflame discontent among the ignorant, it would be practically impossible to prevent the National Congress and its ramifications from becoming a deadly engine of sedition.

What then will be its effect when the leaders of this Congress, the authorised official heads, publish in their authorised official volumes, and throw broadcast over the land, as an example to their followers in every district, literature of an actively incendiary nature ? At the end of the report of the National Congress is printed a pamphlet which, I am told, has been largely circulated in the vernacular, in which case a certain number of potential mutineers has probably been already created by it. I shall make some extracts from this poisonous tract, but I can, in so short a space, give no adequate notion of the amount of venom hidden in it. I request all who take an interest in public affairs, and in the future of this glorious country and of its gifted peoples, to purchase a copy of the report and study the tract for themselves. It represents a hypothetical conversation between a Congresswalla (a Maulvi!) and a peasant. The Congresswalla points to the difference in prosperity between two villages—one *Shamshpur*, which is owned jointly by the villagers, and another *Kambakhtpur*, owned by an absentee Raja. The former is said to typify India as it would be under a native representative government, and the latter, India as it is under British rule. A vivid contrast is drawn between the prosperity of Shamshpur and the misery of Kambakhtpur. Every misfortune from which our poor peasants suffer, whether removable by Government or beyond the resources of human power to cure— the poverty, the extortions of the money-lender, the oppression of the police, the ill-effects of canal water —are described with studied accuracy as ruining Kambakhtpur, while from all of them Shamshpur is free. With such illusions did Jack Cade urge on his band of rebels. I will now quote :—

Maulvi Fariduddin :—" But how does your village thrive ?"

Rambaksh :—" How does it thrive ? Why, Maulvi Sahib, you know that there never is a day but that there is some case from Kambakhtpur in Court ; that we are growing poorer and poorer ; that land is going out of cultivation ; that we have scarcely

oxen enough to plough what we still till.   Look
down the street ; why the houses are half of them
nearly in ruins, and the two *abkari* shops that the
Sirkar has set up here are always full.   Even this
chopal, built by our forefathers and so much needed
for our meetings and our guests, is now in ruins.
Look at Shamshpur.   It is twice as populous as this
bustee (village), and yet there is no *abkari* shop
there, and the *lumbardar* says there never shall
be, and so say they all.   Thrive indeed !   Of all the
miserable places in this whole zila, Kambakhtpur
is nearly one of the worst."

Thus the British Government is charged with
making the people drunk by its liquor policy ; to its
door is laid the poverty of the peasantry ; and re-
gardless of facts, it is said that the poverty of the
country is increasing, and the land is passing out of
cultivation.

Further on, English officials, as a class, are thus
described :—" They don't know the difference between a 6-anna crop and a 16-anna crop, and press
in bad times for rent, so that we have to sell our
cattle ; they don't know who is reliable (*matbir*), and
they make advances, when none ought to be given,
to ne'er-do-weels that lose their money, and then say
we are *all budmashes* (bad characters, rogues), and
won't even give seed-grain to the best of us, when
times are such that we really need it.   And then
they are fussy and self-conceited, and won't hear a
word from any of us.   There was the old tank there,
the Soorujkund, that from generation to generation

used to irrigate half the village ; that burst when I
was a boy fifty years ago. Well, we wanted the
Raja to repair this.   It wouldn't have cost many
hundred rupees, and the whole village knew from
their forefathers how well it worked. But no !
Naib Sahib knew better ; he wouldn't listen to us.
' What you cattle-folk know ?   Hold your tongues.'
He was all for new-fangled plans.   He would bring
a *kul* (channel) of the *Sirkari* canal to irrigate the
village.   We told him that canal water is cold, that
our land lay low, that it would not do.   But what
was the use ? ' What you cattle-folk know ?   Hold
your tongues ;' and so the *kul* was brought, and
the first year it overflowed and swamped half the
crops, and then when the water dried up the canal
people came and measured up all the land, and
made us pay tax for ' one watering.' A fine thing,
seeing it had ruined our crops. But we had to
pay, and now it is bringing the *reh* (a saline
efflorescence) all over our best lands. The Raja
pays no heed to us ; his naibs understand nothing
of our affairs.   They order this and order that, press
us for money in season and out of season, they
know nothing of village matters themselves, and
they won't hear a word from us because they think
they are all-wise and we utter fools—and under
such a system (*dastur*), how can a village be otherwise than ruined ?"

Thus, even our benevolent efforts to avert
famine by means of irrigation are used as a dagger
wherewith to stab us. I will close my extracts with

the following charming description of an English Collector, Mr. Zabardast:—

Rambaksh :—"Remember him ? Ram, Ram, *'ska nam mut lo* (don't mention him) ; I bear his marks now (where I can't show them to you, Maulvi Sahib), though it is twenty years ago. You see, his *lashkar* (camp) came to our village. There was no grass for the horses ; the Collector shouted to the Tahsildar, who said Rambaksh was responsible. ' Oh,' said the Sahib, striking me with his whip. ' You are the son of a pig, the misbegotten (*suar ka bacha, haram-zada*). I'll teach you how to attend to orders. Here, *khlassi* (tent-pitcher), tie him up and give him thirty *baints* (blows with a cane), and lay it well on.' Now the Tahsildar had never spoken a word to me about the matter. I tried to explain this, but the Sahib hit me over the mouth and face with his whip, shouting out ' hold your tongue. I'll teach you ! Tie him up, tie him up, flog his life out ;' and I was dragged away and flogged till I became insensible. It was a month before I could walk. Yes, he was a bad one ; many Collectors have I known—some good, some indifferent—but this was the only real devil."

Now what does this mean, and what will it lead to ? It means—if Government allows this sort of propaganda to go on—it means the massacre of Englishmen, and their wives and children. For on what material is this seditious trash thrown ? Not on the educated and cultured. Not on those who owe their means of livelihood to British rule, and

who would be swept away at once if it went.   Not
on men who are afraid of fighting.   The people of
these Provinces are not cowards ; they love a fight
as well almost as an Englishman.   We had examples
at Delhi and Etawah.   And some classes of these
people, notably the Muhammadan and the Thakur,
the most spirited and pugnacious, have lost terribly
by the turn in the political kaleidoscope.   Religious
fanaticism is not yet dead.   And the poverty of the
whole Muhammadan community and of the noble
families is so distressing, and their backwardness in
English education is so great, that only a Government which was the slave of noise or doctrinaire
theories would frame measures in disregard of it.
Now if they are urged to dwell on their sorrows,
which are invariably laid to the British Government,
instead of trying to improve themselves by trade
and education, the result will be that disloyalty will
take its seat in their hearts.   Do you think they
will stop at reform of the Legislative Councils ?
And do you think the Congress people, who have
stirred up these passions, can allay them ?   They
would be blown away as butterflies in a hurricane.

The worst sufferers by a mutiny would be
Muhammadans.   As far as savagery goes, both sides
would have a good fling.   At such a period men
become fiends, and the innocent and the guilty, the
strong and the defenceless, share the same fate.
The English nation, on whose benevolence at home
the Congresswallas lay such stress, would forget all
about constitutions and elective councils, and cry

only for vengeance.   But England would not lose her
national existence, while the Muhammadan would
be irretrievably ruined.   This is why the Muhammadan leaders wish to keep their people from the
whirlpool of political agitation.   My revered chief,
Sir Syed Ahmed, whose humble disciple in matters
political I boast myself, has pointed this out clearly.
No one has even grappled with his arguments, but
in place of reason a shower of mud and abuse has
been hurled at him ever since.   He has been called
selfish, foolish, childish, and a flatterer.   But the
fact is, people in other Provinces and of other nations can in no way understand the circumstances
and feelings of the people here.   The Bengali has
made enormous progress under British rule ; his
political star is in the ascendant ; how can he
put himself in the position of the Musalman
whose greatness is in the past, and who sees ruin
staring him in the face?   If, in spite of this, he
will disseminate his poisonous literature among
Muhammadans, have not Muhammadan patriots a
right to be angry?   In Bengal, Madras, and Bombay,
there was no mutiny, though, if report be right,
materials exist for one in the last of these Provinces.
To people there it seems an unreality, a chimera.
But it is far otherwise here.   Our old men were
middle aged in 1857.   The *Bombay Gazette* urged
the Muhammadans of the N.-W. P. to indulge in
a little " wholesome grumbling," if they could find
anything to grumble about.   Pray how, if we start
grumbling, are we to be sure that it will remain

" wholesome ? " There is plenty for Muhammadans
to grumble at.   This so-called self-Government of
the municipalities, in which Muhammadans have
been bound hand and foot and handed over to their
rivals to be governed by them, is a case in point.
An order just issued by the Bengal Government
that all minor appointments are to be given by
competitive examination—an order which will almost
destroy the Muhammadan middle-class which cannot
for one generation at least acquire English education sufficient to compete with others—is another.
But rather than bring these things forward and
create a popular agitation, we will submit to them
as the lesser evil. Another Syed Ahmed, the
great Wahabi, and Maulvi Ismail, his supporter,
raised a great popular agitation, but urged their
followers never to attack the British.   They fought
the Sikhs, but after that what took place ?   To
every thoughtful Muhammadan the idea of another
mutiny is as horrible, more horrible I believe than
to an Englishman, and to every Musalman lady
more dreadful even than to an English lady.

I have written the above on the supposition
that the promoters of this movement have no
desire of raising a storm, but are doing it unwit-
tingly, not knowing the country.   But this is by no
means as certain as it at first sight appears.   In
the report of the Congress, after many eloquent
harangues on urging forward " the chariot of India's
destined development," there comes with a sense
of infinite relief a speech by a man, Babu Ambica

Charan Muzamdar, who had the courage to express opinions distasteful to the majority. He said :—
" There is a kind of maniacal writing in many of the petty Vernacular papers that would qualify, and should qualify, the writers for prison diet." But he was shouted down. This is a small incident. It would not be fair to press it too far. Of very much more serious account as showing the *conscious* drift of the movement is a pamphlet written by Mr. Hume, " The Father of the Congress," entitled *The Star in the East*. At the close are printed some articles from the *Indian Mirror*, evidently written by the same hand ; but whether written by him or not, printed and sanctioned by him in this pamphlet. These letters are actively and consciously seditious. No one but a madman would have written them if he did not wish to bring the people to the verge of rebellion. I make the following quotation :—

" We again quote Mr. Payne :—' The settlers (at Cape Colony) petitioned for representative government in 1841, but their claims were neglected (*they took no measures to make themselves disagreeable*), and so little attention was paid to their wishes that the Home Government, when the Australians refused to take any more convicts, determined to make the Cape a penal settlement, and in 1849 despatched a ship-load of convicts to Cape Town. The colonists, who were resolved to make a stand, rose in arms and refused to allow them to be landed. This incident fixed their claims on public attention,

and in the next year (1850) the Governor was em-
powered to summon a constituent council for the
purpose of settling a more acceptable form of
government.'

"Full responsible Government was then con-
ceded, and though their path, in other ways, has
been beset with thorns, this was the end of the
colonists' troubles with their Government.

"Now, can anything show more clearly than
this simple, unvarnished story that the whole secret
of eliciting reform at the hands of our good Lord
and Master, John Bull, is to make oneself disagreeable? You may apparently complain and petition *ad
infinitum ;* thus did the Canadians, the Australians
and the Cape, but they took nothing by their
motions ; they might shout until they were hoarse,
but until they began to kick, to fight, or evince a
readiness to do so—until, in fact, they began to
make themselves disagreeable in good earnest—no
one paid the slightest attention to them.

"Very clearly we have to make ourselves disagreeable, and please God, as time goes on, we will
do so, and no mistake. But there are ways and
ways of doing things. We do not approve of a
resort to arms. We shall not break either the laws
of God or man. We shall work within both constitutional and common law and local law limits,
but we shall nevertheless hope to make ourselves
ultimately so stupendously disagreeable as to force
even our claims on public attention, and so secure
those modifications in the existing form of the

administration which are essential to the prosperity of India, and the well-being of her now greatly depressed and suffering population."

He also quotes Canada as rising in arms, praises the Canadians for it, and says Indians must take this lesson to heart, but not rise in arms. However, if freedom of the Press and the right to agitate be interfered with, he says :—" *We* also may begin to think of sterner measures to vindicate our rights." Is this direct incentive to mutiny or not ? Does it or does it not tend to a repetition of those scenes at which the whole world shuddered ? He brings forward examples of colonies which have gained the identical proposals of the National Congress after, and only after, an appeal to arms. He lays the greatest emphasis on this again and again, and tells his followers to take the lesson of the colonies to heart. He tells the people of India to take the first steps towards this rebellion, and to make themselves " stupendously disagreeable." He says there are other ways of accomplishing this without an appeal to arms, but he does not say what those ways are. Then he says it would be wrong for Indians to mutiny ; but he does not explain why it was right in the colonists, as he positively asserts it was, and would be wrong in the people of India. Now Mr. Hume may wish us to believe that the sentence, telling the people of India not to appeal to arms, is a proof that there is nothing seditious in his intentions. It is nothing of the sort. To have ended the reasoning with the natural conclusion and exhortation to revolt, would have been absolute treason, and would have brought Mr. Hume within the compass of the law. Therefore he gives all the steps of the reasoning and leaves his readers to draw the right conclusion, himself cleverly ending up with an illogical statement by which he seeks to evade the direct charge of treason. No man who really wished to keep the people quiet, and to dispel notions of revolt, would have held up the picture of countries which had gained what they wanted by revolt. A man who wants to cure a drunkard does not place a glass of brandy on the table before him, deliver an oration on the delight of its flavour, tell him he can have it by stretching out his hand, and that many people have derived the greatest benefit from drinking brandy, but that, under present circumstances, it would be wiser if he abstained.

Furthermore, he insinuates that the people ought to mutiny if freedom of the Press and the right to agitate be removed. Why freedom of the Press and the right to agitate in particular? No one but an Englishman would have singled out those two things as the only causes justifying a rebellion. There are many things an Oriental cares infinitely more about—his religion, for example. And would not anyone, Oriental or not, care more about the alleged poverty of the country—not to mention the castigations of Mr. Zabardast? A Press Act would be no grievance to the people in Kambakhtpur; may they not rise for their many grievances which he is so careful to point out to them? And even if a Press

Act be the greatest evil the people of India could suffer, is it not dangerous morality to teach them that they have the right to rebel? Perhaps, indeed, Government will not carry its mania for license of the Press to such an extent as to allow active incentives to revolt. Will Mr. Hume then be ready to stand by his words? Let him head the Congress and die the death of a martyr, with as many Congresswallas as he can get to stand by him! But let him not stir up the Mahomedan and the Thakur to their ruin.

All this that I have said may appear to English ears very unwarranted by the circumstances. I don't think it will so appear to the ears of my Hindustani countrymen. Everything looks quiet and peaceable. Popular agitation flourishes in England and nothing bad takes place. Yes; but England is not a conquered people under foreign rule. And, moreover, the people there is king. Popular agitation is nothing more than the working of the king's mind. The constitution at once brings into effect the people's wishes. But to talk of a " constitutional agitation" when there is, and can be, no constitution, is a perversion of language. And agitation without a constitution to work it off on is the prelude of bloodshed. Look at Ireland. And popular agitation in India will inevitably end in its becoming another Ireland on a much larger scale. We live apart from the people, and we take little trouble to see what is going on. The thing is still in its infancy and could be checked. The virus has not yet spread far in these Provinces. But after a time it will be very difficult to check it. It is no proof that because things are smooth and quiet there is no danger. How was the Mutiny of 1857 ushered in? The Anglo-Indian world up to the hour when the great tragedy burst upon them was busily amusing itself as best it can in this country with social nothings. And what were the causes of this Mutiny? The generally assigned cause is that the people feared their religion was about to be touched by Government. This National Congress is not a religious business. But religion is not the only thing which affects men. Poverty is as strong a provocative of crime as anything else. Mr. Dadabhai Nowroji is diligently trying to prove that India is growing poorer. This can produce no harm in his own community, who live like princes and are a thousand times as rich as they used to be. But on nations which are really impoverished it may produce deadly effects. A political cause is also given for the great Mutiny—the annexation of Oudh. If the passions of the people be stirred up about politics, there is no reason why there should not be a mutiny. The soldiery will readily imbibe the sentiments, and then all will be up. Mr. Hume boasted that he and his organisation could reach the soldiers and fill them with their sentiments and ideas. The people will get ready and wait for a favourable opportunity. If there be a single battle lost in a fight with Russia, this will be taken as the signal, and the whole of India will be aflame.

THEODORE BECK.

THE SEDITIOUS PAMPHLET.

Translated from the Urdu Letter of Munshi Imtiaz Ali.

THE supporters of the National Congress have published a pamphlet, which consists of a conversation between two hypothetical personages, Maulvi Fariduddin and Ram Bakhsh, the effect of which, on the hearts of the readers, will be to produce a settled conviction that the English rule exercises a crushing oppression on the people, and that the laws, rules, and administration of the Government are bad, despotic, and ruinous for natives of India. In the last paragraph of the pamphlet the intention is expressed of circulating it in every village and hut in the whole country, and of making every man in India understand its meaning. And further, that over and beyond the circulation of the book, hired men should be engaged, who should travel to every village, and in every way try to make the people understand its meaning.

The contents of the book are such as to produce, without a doubt, on the hearts of the readers, a feeling of opposition to the whole administration of the Government, and to cause in the ignorant a most dangerous excitement of anger and hatred against British rule. Moreover, it raises such new hopes of representative government, and of untold visionary benefits to be derived therefrom, as in all probability will affect the brains of even the educated classes.

The book, besides being printed in the other vernaculars of India, has been published in Lucknow by Ganga Pershad Varma, and the supporters of the National Congress have displayed the greatest energy in its circulation. Subscriptions for printing and distribution have also been raised. If but for a short time this state of things continues, and the supporters of the National Congress be successful in their attempts, then it is certain that the result will be that the whole people of India, with one heart and one tongue, will become hostile to the British Government. When such has become the case, it will be extremely difficult to set things right again. There is thus the greatest danger that from these evil doings of the National Congress a universal discontent will arise, and then it will be impossible for Government in a time of necessity to derive from such discontented subjects any kind of assistance. In such time it will be able to obtain help from those men only who think their own well-being, or ruin, is involved in that of the Government, or who stand at their posts from a sense of duty. But from subjects who want by unlawful force to change the Government, and who hate it, it can expect nothing. And if a time of difficulty on the frontier or with a foreign Power should arise, at that very time they will attempt to create disturbance within.

Perhaps the British Government believes that all the people of India, with one heart and one voice, are pleased with its administration. But such is

not the case.   Many things in the arrangements of
the British Government are liked, but there are also
many matters about which people in different parts
of the country complain.   For some years the ru-
mour has been spreading among the fighting classes
that the Russians are coming ; that they are very
brave, and have regard for brave races ; that they
give very high positions in the army to brave people
without consideration of race or religion ; and that
they will receive much consideration on their coming.   This class of fighting men has suffered greatly,
and many complain of not getting employment.
The class of *Mahajans* * is not opposed to Government on account of peace, nor do they look forward
to the coming of the Russians ; but they look back
with regret to the old *Nawabi* times.† They complain
of the stoppage of the *hundi* business (bills of ex-
change).   They are angry at the money-order system and the opening of Government savings banks
and other English banks.   The people educated in
Hindi, Persian, Sanskrit and Arabic, who used to
make their living as clerks, are generally discontented on account of the middle-class and other examinations, and their being thereby thrown out of employment because they have lost their only means of
livelihood.   The old aristocracy grumble against
the Government for not protecting them from the
abuse they receive at the hands of low upstarts in the
Press, and they long for an opportunity of resorting

---

* Native Bankers.
† Times of the Kings of Oudh, before 1856.

to the good old method of dealing summarily with such offenders. Indian artisans are angry at the introduction of foreign goods and the loss of their art or profession. The people who have received a high English education are discontented because they do not obtain high positions—Memberships of Council, Secretaryships, Lieutenant-Governorships, &c. And some of those people who have gained most from the British Government are loudest in their demonstrations of discontent.

As I am not now criticising the administration of Government, it is not necessary for me to discuss whether the causes of this discontent are justifiable or not. My object is to point out that, before the coming of the National Congress, some sections of the people were rightly or wrongly discontented with the British rule, and that it was desirable, for the good government of India, to consider this discontent and, as far as possible, to remove it, and as regards unavoidable grievances, to instruct in some suitable manner the disaffected people, and by pointing out the impossibility of gratifying their wishes, to make them contented. But pursuing an opposite course, the crowd of English educated people have, by starting the National Congress and printing such pamphlets, adopted a policy the result of which will be that no single native of India will be free from discontent ; and that among those classes in which disaffection already exists, the excitement of hatred will greatly increase. The flames of disloyalty will leap up in the breasts of those ignorant people who are wearily passing their lives in the hope of the arrival of the Russians. Does the National Congress wish by printing such books to spread universal opposition and discontent, and by showing criminal violence to coerce Government into carrying out its wishes? Cannot the National Congress accomplish its objects in a fit and suitable way without employing dangerous methods? Is the National Congress to be allowed exemption from obedience to the law of the land, that it can carry on its proceedings so fearlessly?

Inasmuch as I have with my own eyes seen the Mutiny of 1857, and have suffered terrible losses and troubles in those times, and for one year and some months lived a life that was worse than death, I have the greatest fear that by the widespread circulation of this book and by the methods of the National Congress a great mutiny will arise. I speak as one who remembers how we were looted, first by the mutineers and next by the British troops ; how we sat in our houses and were robbed of everything, even to our clothing ; how the food was stolen, and such as could not be taken away was destroyed. The first night eight of us had to sleep under one blanket, and for four or five days we almost died of starvation. I appeal to Government to protect us from a repetition of such horrors. The effect of the Mutiny of 1857 was limited to the N.-W. P. and Oudh, but if from the doings of the National Congress any mutiny arise, it will spread all over India. No doubt the power and greatness of the British

Government will find no difficulty in suppressing it ; but it cannot be done without fresh loss to the lives and property of the people, and to the army of Government. The reputation of the British Government will be stained. The progress of everything will receive the greatest blow, and for a long time the condition of India will be wretched and miserable. On this account I bring this matter to the attention of the Government and of its officials.

IMTIAZ ALI.

TRANSLATION OF A LECTURE

Delivered by His Highness the Maharaja of Benares,
G. C. S. I., Patron of the Benares Institute,
at the Town Hall, on 20th July, 1888.

BROTHERS.—You well know that I am not
in the habit of talking at any length or creating any excitement needlessly ; but as Sa'di says :—
" If I see a blind man going towards a well and
be silent, it will be a sin ; " so, acting on this
proverb, I am about now to address a few words
to you.

I see that some of my countrymen (how sad
for me to confess it) are trying to bring endless
calamity, disgrace, and ruin to their country.   I also
am an inhabitant of dear India, though one of its
humblest, but I would certainly not like to fall into
the well ; if you all choose to do so, why—you
must bear the brunt of it.   In the Benares Institute, according to a saying, " secrets of politics are
known only to rulers, " so that any discussion of them
is against the standing rules ; but when the Institute
itself ceases to exist, of what purpose would the
rules then be ? " Necessity has no law ; " and " to
escape death all is lawful ; " these are two well-worn
proverbs.   As we all sail in the same boat, so brothers self-protection must be looked for above all
other matters.   But to the point :—

I hear that some people have perpetrated a
chimera, and named it " The National Congress ! "

National Congress—delegate—representative government—I myself really do not understand the
meaning of these words ; therefore I cannot explain
them to you in my own language. Hitherto I understood that "delegate" meant a deputy, an agent or a
representative; but I see in the newspapers that some
"delegates" from Benares were present at the Madras
meeting. Now, I have questioned several, and cannot find out any who would acknowledge having
sent a deputy, agent or representative from Benares
to Madras ; or whether any recorded proxy was so
delegated. So the saying has been verified that
" whether you acknowledge or not I am your guest."
Let those who choose give what meaning they
like to the word "delegate" by which they may
probably mean a ghost or demon, a genii or mortal
man ; but our purpose is to ascertain what the
so-called National Congress wants and what its
objects are.

I know very well that there are some men in
the Congress whose equals we can scarcely find, and
their motives are also good and pure ; but saints
cannot always make good statesmen. Dadhichi
gave even his thigh-bone to get off the task of Government, and if you say among the Congress party
there are men holding the degree of B. A. or M. A.,
why I can only remind you that Dr. Ballantyne
styled such persons "unfledged birds." As far as I
understand, these simple-hearted people want a
"representative government," perhaps like that of
America. Though they may not just now confess

this openly, yet they—and mark the inconsistency —while holding these views which are opposed to the policy of Government, do not cease to pray constantly for Her Most Gracious Majesty, whose loyal subjects they profess to be ! But if they have any common sense they will try, as the saying goes, " to take hold of the arms by taking hold of the fingers," and they will lay first of all a firm foundation ; because if such be not their object, then what is it ? No sane man with a head on his shoulders will take so much trouble and make so much fuss without having some object in view. If you say that the Congress wants only to represent to the Government true facts and to give better advice, and that they do not think of bringing any pressure, then why do they make such unseemly noise and raise such an agitation ? Cannot a man even now bring to the notice of the Government any matter he likes, or give the Government any advice he chooses ? Why are there so many newspapers ? The Government will be most thankful for any observations which will tend to promote the welfare of the people, and it will immediately act upon any suggestions which tend to promote this object. Look at the Civil Court. It was this very Court which the then reigning Maharaja Kapurthala told Mr. Thomason was the Court of Lunatics (Divani means Civil and Divana a lunatic), and I will show you what he meant by an illustration. A gentleman of this city had sued another gentleman for Rs. 4,500. The suit was actuated, I must inform you, by motives of malice because the native gentleman in question was security for a European. The case went on for 18 long years. Both parties died, and then at last the decree was passed against the son of the defendant for Rs. 26,000, but through the intercession of mutual friends and fear of an appeal to England Rs. 6,500 were accepted, and a deed of release was given by the plaintiff's son. Now the Civil Court has become proverbial for speed : for accuracy I cannot vouch. A man returned home from the Allahabad fair ; the people asked him for a descriptive account of what he had seen. He said, brothers ! don't ask anything about the railway trains, the cholera pestilence, and the *decisions of the Small Cause Courts !*

Might I now call your attention for a few minutes to the progress of events during the last century. Warren Hastings came here from Calcutta in sailing boats. No one had up to that time seen a steamer. Modes of conveyance were then crude, and it took a friend of mine and his father, 55 years ago, to reach Agra *viâ* Etawah in bullock carts and palkis, a month or so. Not to speak of railways, the time I refer to was when even the Grand Trunk Road was not in existence. Now, coming to our own time, I think no one will deny that the Railway and the Telegraph have added considerably to the convenience, welfare, and prosperity of the inhabitants. So that one might well say that a year's life now is far more valuable and useful than that of a 100 years before the British rule. Allow me to ask you whether all these blessings have been brought to our dear country by this or any other similar Congress. You ought to enquire of these *Congresswallas* what the relative and numerical positions of the educated in America and India are. An American woman holding a similar position to that which maid-servants and nurses occupy in India I have often seen, and such can "cut the ears" of many of our Babu Sahibs and Thakur Sahibs, whom she can teach in all respects for years to come. Another point is, can you tell me how much gentlemen of your position in England spend in educating their children and how much you similarly spend here? In Germany, education and military service are compulsory: would you like such a system to be legally enforced here. Schools have been established in India, but we all know how loth the Babus and Thakurs are to send their children to these institutions for education, and it is wonderful if even one per cent. of the population avail themselves of the educational means placed within their reach. There is an English proverb, "first deserve then desire." I cannot recall just now anything like it in our language. But I can assure you, and that without hesitation, that our kind Government is always anxious to permit us to have a share in the administration, and that as it finds the opportunity, it invites us to do so.

But these matters are perhaps beyond your comprehension. Now, as regards the Indian Council, you will remember that men like Maharaja

Scindhia and Maharaja Patiala were the first to be admitted. But they considered the serving in the Council an unbearable nuisance, and the Nawab of Rampur on being subsequently elected, after remain-ing some weeks in Calcutta, feigned sickness and returned home, telling the Viceroy that there was wisdom in all his acts with the exception of his selec-tion of Calcutta as his capital. A poet has truly said that " Calcutta has been built on a piece of land from hell itself. " Now, it is a well-known fact that every man is not fit for every business. Eng-lish Dukes, Earls, and Marquises, many of whom have larger incomes than many of our Maharajas and Nawabs, feel that it is incumbent on them to attend the British Parliament. But apart from all this, there is an Association which has deservedly received the recognition of the Viceroy, who clearly saw that there was no better representative of India than the British Indian Association in Calcutta. The National Congress cannot equal even the dust off the feet of that noble Association. Though an oilman by caste, yet the Viceroy selected the able and energetic Secretary of that Association, Babu Krishna Das Pal, in whose place we have an efficient substitute in Raja Peary Mohan Mukerji. But a heterogeneous mass is now thrusting itself forward, and in order to obtain seats in the Durbar and to rub their shoulders with the Rajas, even *Kalvars* and *Mochis* are leaving no stone unturned to be elected as Municipal Commissioners, or to be appointed Honorary Magistrates. You can judge of the work

of our countrymen by taking into consideration only
that done by the Benares Municipality. You may
remember what Mr. F. B. Gubbins, Magistrate of
Benares, did single-handed for the City, and what
the Board now, notwithstanding its countless taxes,
is in vain endeavouring likewise to do. You may
say whatever you like, but, as far as I understand,
the real object of these *Congresswallas* is to have a
majority of natives in the Imperial Legislative
Council, in order that, when the question of an increase arises owing to some sudden and unexpected
cause, the native members of the Council may have
the opportunity of displaying their ideas of government by proposing instead of an increase a reduction in expenditure and the abolition of the Income
Tax. For example, they may recommend the
reduction of the European soldiers here and the
raising of a native Volunteer Corps, or the appoint-
ment of native Commissioned Officers in the Army;
but if the Government has even a particle of sense
left it must, in order to secure peace and harmony,
increase the European soldiery in proportion to the
numerical strength of the native armed men ; and
so with the expenses. The Government cannot
forget the year 1857, at least for the next two thousand years. As an illustration of military zeal and
duty, see how the Duke of Connaught is discharging
the duties of a Commander-in-Chief, and how the
Maharaja Kashmir discharged his duties when he
was appointed General of the British Armies. The
son of the French Emperor, Louis Napoleon, went

to Zululand as a Volunteer. There is just now
some disturbance again in that land. If the *Congresswallas* give me a list of their sons, I can send
such a list to the higher authorities, who would probably post these men to Zululand as Volunteers! or
perhaps our wise native legislators may propose to
do away with the highly-paid Covenanted Commissioners, Judges, and Magistrates, and put in their
places low-paid natives or honorary functionaries.
But, just for one moment, let me draw your attention
to one body of our armed men, the Native Police ;
does not their utter inefficiency almost lead you to
wish that European constables should be in every
station. I would never be surprised if our Native
Police some day reported us to be rebels and revolt-
ers. If you say that the Congress does not want a
majority in the Council, then remaining in the
minority, even if we be 500 strong, of what use can
we be. But there is another aspect of affairs to look
at. Suppose the Government do admit as many
native members by election as are now nominated
into the Council, I ask you how would you care to
have *Kalvars* and *Mochis* as our legislators. The
shoemaker can never get beyond his last, nor the
brewer beyond the still : so there must be disturbances in one way or the other.

Democracy is an occidental idea. A Hindu
cannot comprehend it as long as he is a Hindu. It
is against his religious belief. The divisions of
Varna are the basis of his religion. He cannot see
without distress a Brahman or Kshtriya serving a

Sudra.   A Brahman may beg or even may die, yet he will never touch a dish from which a Sudra has partaken food.   When to save themselves from the hands of the Muhammadans the Mahrattas formed a union among themselves, they appointed a Brahman their Peshwa (leader), Baji Rao.   So long as Hindus remain in Hindustan you cannot succeed in extending the democratical ideas.   If there is any defect in our Government, it is only this that our Government is democratical, inasmuch as it appoints its officials by the result of examinations passed for official posts, independent of the *social* position of the candidate.   For example, we may have a carpenter as Deputy Collector, and a Kalvar Honorary Magistrate.   The Congress men want a separation of the Executive from the Judicial and technical education.   This is a very small affair. Hundreds of proposals like this come before the Government every day, and hundreds of changes which are thought an improvement are always being made.   About education—who prevents you ?   You can teach your sons in your schools to read Milton and Shakespeare, or to draw pictures, or (if the worst comes to the worst) to parch grain.   The choice lies with you.   Why do not these *Congresswallas* go to some Native State and turn it into an administrative model according to their fancies.   Babu Nilambar Mukerji has been in Kashmir, and perhaps a brother of the Indian Mirror is still in Jeypur.   Why has the Nizam of Hyderabad appointed Colonel Marshal his Secretary, and why has the Begam of Bhupal

appointed Colonel Ward her Manager? Some of
the advocates of the Congress bring forward the
names of some British officers as being in their
favour; but these latter are and cannot but be disappointed Civilians. If a native feels disappointed
because he is not made a Judge in the High Court
or a Dewan in a Native State, is it any wonder that
a British Officer feels disappointed if he be not
made a member of the Viceregal Council or a
Lieutenant-Governor of the Province, especially
when they both think themselves equally fit for
the posts aspired to.

It is much to be regretted that people in England do not know the real state of affairs in India,
nor the peculiar nature and habits of the Indians.
One lady actually regretted that the Indian cultivators could not provide themselves with boots !!!
(what an idiosyncrasy); another had a long conversation with a Rani on the evil effects of infant
marriage, and was surprised to hear that the Rani
had been married at the age of seven and had sons
and grandsons, all of whom were happy and contented. The Rani then turned to the lady and observed
that her hair was turning grey, and inquired
whether no one had ever offered her proposals of
marriage, and she suggested that English laws re-
quire some modification which would ensure ladies
against remaining so long in the state of single
blessedness. Self-interested persons ignorant on
Indian matters not only mislead the leading Members of Parliament, but they rush into print on the

slightest pretext, and ventilate what they call the
grievances of the Indians, and thus increase the difficulties of the Indian Government.   In the Western
countries as the Ministers resign when their budget
is not passed, so here in India the Viceroy must
resign ; and if you ask whether there is no native fit
for that post, I say leave the question of fitness aside;
without the British protection two French Regi-
ments from Chandernagore are quite enough to
plunder Calcutta, and to conquer India up to Peshawar.   If our Government had not taken Burmah it
had become probably the property of the French ;
and even if the French did not come, Amir Abdul
Rahman Khan with his ten thousand horsemen can
plunder and massacre down to Madras.   It is said
that the Jats and Mahrattas have 700,000 horsemen
at Panipat, but Ahmad Shah Durrani scattered
them away with his handful of cavalry.   In short,
as I have already said, had these *Congresswallas*
followed the tracks, step by step, as chalked out
by the British Indian Association, they would
have been most likely benefactors of their country ; but the track which they have followed
now and the fuss they are making, and the articles they are publishing in the Vernacular newspapers, and the speeches they are making to the
ignorant masses, coupled with the mischievous
pamphlets they are distributing, must convey to the
ignorant masses the idea that the natives will get
high salaries ; that they will be appointed to those
posts which are now held by Europeans ; that the

service will increase, and more pay will be obtained ;
and that the taxes will be abolished—if not abolished
they must be reduced ; as Babu Harish Chandra
had his motto here in his Kavibachan-Sudha—
" let the disease of taxation be swept away"
(*kardukh bahai*). Who likes to pay a tax ? More
than any one I personally shall be glad if this
word " tax " be cut out from the dictionary ;
but you are to remember if there be no tax there
would be no government, and then might will
be right.

In my humble opinion if the Government will
not take the trouble in some shape or other to put
down these mischievous movements and writings,
no doubt sooner or later the minds of the ignorant
masses will be, to a certain extent, prejudiced against
them, and disturbances may take place in the
country. Then we must suffer and be ruined.
Though the Hindus blame the Muhammadans and
the Muhammadans blame the Hindus for the failure
of the plan, yet they both acknowledge more or less
their failure. The blister has burst, and the more you
scratch it now the worse it will be. The Government any how will not suffer. The Government will
be the gainer in every way ; whether the melon falls
on the knife or the knife on the melon, the melon must
suffer. But, in conclusion, I ask you to bear in mind
one thing most clearly. It is far from my intention
to insult in any way any oilman or carpenter or
Kalvar or Mochi, but I have endeavoured simply to
prove that democracy or representative government

does not suit India, and that elections will not do for the Council. Oh Almighty God, I pray, give some wisdom to our Hindu and Muhammadan brethren, that they may close up this Congress business, and not prolong the quarrel which can have but one inevitable and disastrous end.

———

MR. SYED HOSAIN BILGRAMI

ON

THE NATIONAL CONGRESS.

Nawab Imad-ud-Daulah, Maulvi Syed Hosain Bilgrami, Ali Yar Khan Bahadur, Motamin Jung, Secretary of the Council of State of His Highness the Nizam, has written the following letter with respect to the Indian Patriotic Association to the Honorable Sir Syed Ahmed, Khan Bahadur, Secretary of the Association :—

MY DEAR SIR SYED AHMED,—I am glad to see that you have laid the foundation of the Indian Patriotic Association in opposition to the so-called Indian National Congress. I have long been of opinion that it was high time for some such movement, and when Mr. Beck was on a visit here, I had the pleasure of discussing with him the urgent need of a conservative organisation for the purpose of banding together such of our fellow-subjects— Hindus, Muhammadans and Christians—as in common with us deplored the spirit of unrest with which *soi-disant* patriots were inoculating the country, and wished to preserve the existing social and political order from violent disruption at their hands. The scope of the movement which we discussed was, however, wider than a mere opposition to the Indian National Congress, and was to have embraced a free dissemination of conservative views

in politics and religion, and exposure of the fallacy
underlying the transfer of a democratic propaganda
to India with all its latent dangers.   The movement
could not have been initiated by an abler or a more
worthy leader than yourself.

While cordially agreeing with you in your
general attitude towards the question, and placing
my services, such as they may be, at your disposal
in furtherance of the objects of the association you
have founded, and of which I hope you will do me
the honor of enrolling me as a member, I beg to
offer a few general observations on the principles
which, with some minor exceptions, I am proud of
sharing with you.

I take it as axiomatic that Britain has a civilis-
ing Mission in India, and that in our own best interests British power must be upheld at all costs.
The good time (if it ever comes) when India will
have lived long enough under a self-governing people to have herself acquired the art of self-government, and above all, that of self-defence, is so far
distant that it may be omitted from our calculation ;
and it may safely be assumed that we are destined
to live and die under the present *régime* for genera-
tions to come.   Our *soi-disant* patriots themselves
admit that the Empire of England in India must
be upheld, but by a subtle trick of reasoning they
wish to make it out that a loyal attitude towards
the throne is consistent with a seditious abuse of
the administration.   "We would change the system,"
they seem to say, " not the sovereign ; we attack

their measures, not our rulers." They forget that
we are not living on English or American soil, and
that any step that tends in the slightest degree to
weaken the absolute power of the Government,
strikes at the root of England's usefulness to this
Empire. The Imperial Government could not
suffer an Ireland in India and live. It could no
more tolerate a Parnell than it could tolerate another rebellion like that of 1857. Yet so different
are the conditions of political existence in the two
countries, that England not only lives alongside a
discontented Ireland, but it takes Parnell and his
associates to her bosom as trusted counsellors. An
Indian Gladstone would be given short shrift here,
and people would say "serve him right;" and yet
Gladstone is in England an honored (though just
now a rather discredited) name, and one of the first
and foremost of the day.

There would be some show of reason for feeling aggrieved, if legislation in India were under-
taken without regard to the views and wishes of the
people, if our best interests were sacrificed to their
own selfish ends by our rulers, and if the immense
military power possessed by England was wielded
only to grind us down in order to furnish grist for
her own mill. But such is not the case. The Imperial Government undertakes no new measure
without putting itself in possession of the views and
wishes of the people in a manner much more complete and effective than any representative chamber,
such as our patriots sigh for, could supply. We really

enjoy all the advantages of a representative system without the drawbacks with which it would be hampered, if imported into this country—the only difference being that our Government very considerately places it out of our power to make politics a profession. From the way in which our supposed political grievances are paraded by the patriots, one would think that they had just emerged from the workshop of social reform, and with hands yet reeking with the grit of the *débris* of social evils they had helped to demolish, they were about to build up for themselves the fabric of a new political life resplendent with all the glory of a recovered Heaven. But what are the facts of the case ? The facts simply are that the alien Government whom we undertake to teach the art of government, suppressed the more shameful and cruel of those evils out of pure humanity, in the face of strong opposition, open or covert, from the very people whom they concerned, and recently offered to remedy some other crying social evils, which same offer was rejected by our patriots with indignation and scorn.

Ask those who have had to deal with masses of men in India and have helped in governing them, what the effect on the progress and prosperity of the country would be of the introduction of a measure that puts it in the power of any native legislator from his place on the Viceroy's Council to call the Lieutenant-Governor of the Punjab or the Governor of Bombay to account regarding his conduct as a ruler. They will at once tell us that were such a privilege granted there would be an end of the prestige of the Government, and the wondering awe and reverence with which it is regarded by the populace, and which serve the purpose of bulwarks and safeguards to the Empire, would be swept away. Muhamadans among whom the traditions of Empire and its high *devoir* are not yet extinct, ought to understand the importance of this sentiment as a factor of orderly Government. Those who have a stake in the country and have something to lose in the general upheaval apprehended from the spread of democratic tendencies which have no home in this country, ought to appreciate to the full the importance of keeping supreme power intact and untouched, and hedging it round with as much of the elements of awe and reverence as can be saved out of the wreck of old ideas and traditions which are in the process of being ruthlessly destroyed by a blind, ill-judged, and ill-digested imitation of European radicalism.

I hope you will pardon my saying that I do not think Muhammadans have anything especial to dread from the so-called National Congress movement that is not shared by their Hindu fellow-subjects. The danger is a common danger, and if I am able to read it rightly, it consists not so much in what the Congress might do, as in what it tends to undo. We, orientals, are a restful people, our movements are sluggish, our progress in civilisation has followed a slow process of development. This characteristic is an element of our nature, perhaps the outcome of

our climate and environment; it is at any rate a
valuable characteristic, seeing that it preserves us
from the sudden and furious social and political
cyclones which have every now and again swept over
the more warm-blooded nationalities. Now, the
Congress movement is an engine for turning this rest
into unrest, and inciting men to seek change for the
sake of change. It teaches people to be dissatisfied
with their present lot and hanker after something
indefinite, the real nature of which the Missionaries
and Apostles of the new creed have themselves
hardly realised. Our self-constituted teachers are
in this, if they but knew it, merely paying a compli-
ment to their English rulers, namely, the compli-
ment of imitation, and nothing more. Just as
some of us love to rig ourselves out in ill-fitting
tail-coats and trousers of doubtful tailoring, and go
into sulks if we are not afterwards asked to parti-
cipate in the social amenities of our European
neighbours, so we pick up the cry of Irish Home
rulers and English Radicals, and are surprised that
we are not invited over, there and then, to sit in the
House of Commons and help to convert the strong
and beneficent Government of our country into a
haphazard rule of platform and party.

I am glad to see that our co-religionists are, on
the whole, sensible enough to see through the movement and avoid the pitfalls with which its path is lined.
The few misguided men who have given in their
adherence are no doubt excusable on account of
their youth and inexperience. It is easy to see how

little real faith even they have in their new creed
by the vituperation and abuse which they find it
necessary to pour over the devoted heads of its
opponents. The cause must be weak indeed which
needs such doubtful advocacy.

It occurs to me here to instance a very recent
display of the sentiment of which the Congress movement is only a mode of expression. You must
have noticed the indecent haste with which some of
our Congressionist papers have seen it fit to rejoice
in public over the misfortunes of Mr. Commissioner
Crawford. It is premature to crow over such a sad
catastrophe for any one, not to say execrable bad
form. Common decency ought to have admonished
them to hold their tongues. A Government that
will dare place a high and influential official like
Mr. Crawford in such a predicament for the sake of
official purity and honor, deserves all sympathy. It
is matter for condolence rather than for rejoicing.
Mr. Crawford's guilt is not proved yet, and all well-
wishers of order and good Government and of the
noble service to which he belongs, will hope and pray
that he may be able to clear his good name. Better
a man of Mr. Crawford's ability and calibre were he
ten thousand times guilty (which I hope he is not,
though I have no personal interest in the matter) than
a hundred such revilers of the existing order of things
as the Congress movement seems to be breeding.

The Government of a great Continent like
India, peopled by a hundred different nationalities,
and embracing a heterogeneous mass of widely

diverging interests, is no schoolboy's joke, and is
not to be mapped out by an assemblage of school-
masters, lawyers, *et hoc genus omne.*   It needs the
guidance of trained statesmen, backed by phalanxes
of armed and disciplined soldiers ready to die for
Empire and Queen. Those who wish to dictate
how India shall be governed, ought to talk at the
head of an army, and with the mouth of cannon
thundering in their flank.   Will the Congress men
rush forward to fight on the frontier for our hearths
and homes when Russian artillery belches forth fire
and shell at our gateway, and threatens to plunge
us once more into that anarchy from which we
have emerged with England's help and God's ?

It   is   impossible   to   criticise   the   Congress
apart from the programme it has adopted.   An institution must stand   or fall   by the quality of its
handiwork.   I wish to speak of the movement and
its chief representatives with all respect.   They are
men of light and leading, seeking no doubt the
good of our common fatherland in the way that
seems to them best.   But frankly, who that reads the
Resolution, for example, on the Arms Act, or on military expenditure, or on the conquest of Burmah, can
help calling in question the statesmanship of those who
have such puerile sentiments to record on important
questions of practical statecraft.   Any member of the
executive service, native or European—for that matter any sensible man with some practical experience
of how the peace is kept in town and country,
and familiar with the machinery employed—would

pronounce the remedy suggested for the Arms Act grievance, if grievance it is, to be unstatesmanlike and impracticable. The Congress Resolution on this subject, were it carried out, would cause more needless irritation and heartburning than was ever caused by the Act itself. The views of the Congress on volunteering are no doubt very loyal; but there are obvious practical difficulties in the way of their ever being carried out, which would have occurred to the orators who spoke at the Congress, if they had by an effort of imagination, which would have cost them nothing, put themselves in the place of their foreign rulers and worked the problem out from that point of view. This same rule of " putting one's self in another's place " before one weighs that other in the balance of approval or disapproval is, by the way, a golden rule, and if applied to Indian politics by the rulers and the ruled, would, I verily believe, be worth many a Representative Chamber to the subject-races and many a National Congress.

In fact, the demands of the Congress have only to be stated in order to bring their absurdity into prominent relief. Shorn of unnecessary verbiage and presented in all their naked audacity, they are :—

(1). Elective Councils with the right of inter-pellation.

(2). Taxation by popular vote.

(3). Access to all appointments in the State, Civil or Military.

(4). Peace and war by national mandate.

And some others of minor importance.

But underlying all the demands, important or unimportant, is the idea of forcing the hands of Government by what is euphemistically styled "constitutional means," but which, translated into ordinary language, means "seditious agitation;" for there is only a thin paper-wall between agitation and sedition.

I need not dwell on the demand for Elective Councils. Government might possibly see its way to the adoption of some modified system of election for certain seats in Council. Personally, I do not believe it will be an improvement on the present constitution. Indeed, I do not see how any electioneering, properly so called, can be conducted in India. I have heard of no suggestion that was not open to grave objection. The idea of native candidates canvassing for seats on the Viceroy's Council, or delivering speeches setting forth their own merits, and holding out promises to possible constituencies, is at first sight so ludicrously opposed to all our notions of the fitness of things, that it is difficult to stop to look at the serious and practical side of the question. It will no doubt be possible to get a few "unfledged birds" (as H. H. the Maharaja of Benares calls them) or some of his famous Kalvars and Mochis, and mightily tickled their vanity will be in the possession of this new toy, this "sally-come-up" of the imported ballot-box. But will they add to the dignity or usefulness of the Council? I am afraid, not. Representation in the true sense of the word there will be none, for our B. A.'s and

M. A.'s who will manage to get elected are not representative men. They only represent a certain class (the English educated) who hold a very infinitesimal place in the census of the country. They are, moreover, poor men ordinarily, though energetic and pushing—hardly the sort of men, for example, whom the Maharaja before mentioned would care to hobnob with (in the metaphorical, Heaven fore-fend, not the literal sense of the word). It is also said of these graduates (of whom I am proud to call myself one, these strictures notwithstanding), that they begin to grind at the mill of competition from so early a stage that they actually know less of their own country than English officials who make a business and a study of it in the course of their duty— that they are more at home in the geography, folk-lore, and history of Great Britain or China than of their own country. I am afraid the indictment is not without a certain amount of truth. That English educated youths manage to alienate the feeling of their less exotically literate fellow-countrymen is to a certain extent also true. I am afraid we have not yet solved the problem of imparting English education to our youths without impairing their usefulness. This will come with a national system of education, based on religion and morality, but we have no time for such trifles now with our hands full of urgent political reforms!

But granted that we get a proper election and unexceptionable representatives, what shall we gain by it except a few more speeches and little more *talkee talkee.*   A small minority leading the Opposition in such a Senate as the Viceroy's Council would serve no purpose that is not served under the present constitution.   A powerful minority would be replete with mischief and embarrassment ; while a majority, that could outvote the Viceroy and his following, would reduce the Queen's Government in India to a protectorate without the right even of levying tribute from the protected country.   If the Opposition could carry with it a European following, the situation would not be improved ; in fact, the mischief in that case would only be rendered more far-reaching.

I need not spin out the argument against placing the "Vote of Supplies" in native hands, and thus putting it in their power to starve out the Government.   If our Universities had given to the world a financial genius or two who could show our rulers how to make the two ends meet, we might have asked with better grace for some share of power over the purse-strings of the State.   But alas ! our modern Todur Muls are yet unborn, and we have not a shred of evidence to show that if called to power, we shall manage the ways and means of the administration better than their present custodians.

The Covenanted Civil Service question has been threshed out by this time, and the final decision on it is even now under deliberation by Government.   The command of our military resources, which the Congress does not ask for except by implication in the other demands, need not be taken *au-serieux.* That the Government should ask our permission before going to war, could only have occurred to some patriot anxious to parade Peace Association platitudes before a delighted audience of schoolboys, in whose craniums the bump of combativeness was conspicuous by its absence.

I have touched briefly on most of the topics that have engaged the attention of the Congress. Their emissaries are abroad preaching what amounts to sedition towards the existing order of things. They are sowing broadcast the seed of future storms and whirlwinds. This raising of vague aspirations and vain hopes is unsettling men's minds. Your Patriotic Association must be up and doing, if the tide is to be stemmed in time ; and you must begin nearer home. Your work here is cut out for you. While "informing the people of England" in the words of your circular, "of the real condition of India by printing pamphlets from time to time," it behoves the Association to take effective steps, both from the platform and the Press, to disabuse people's minds of the glamour cast on them by the false, though attractive, political programme that is being preached, and save our deluded countrymen from stumbling into pitfalls from which there is no escape for those who pursue the Will-o'-the-Wisps misnamed Political Liberty and Popular Government.

It is unfortunate in this connection that your public utterances should have been misunderstood to encourage the banding together of Muhammadans

against Hindus as regards the aims and objects of
the Congress movement. I do not think a man of
your sagacity and experience could have failed to
see that such a view of the matter was a mistake,
both of fact and of strategy. The interest of the
two peoples, rightly understood, are one and in-
divisible. The propagation of a spirit of unrest and
discontent is as pernicious for the one nationality as
for the other, and it behoves them both equally to
unite and make common cause against this movement which has been set on foot by a few ambitious
spirits, and eagerly taken up by the class whose
principal claim to be heard is its blind adoption of
foreign ideas, its familiarity with the tactics of English agitators, and its ill-judged imitation of the
modern European love of change.

The task before you is that of educating native
public opinion into an attitude, not of servile sub-
jection, but of manly sympathy with the Government
and a due appreciation of the difficulties it has to
encounter in the work of keeping order among
the vast and heterogeneous conglomeration of
races and nationalities found in India. The
velocity with which we are progressing would
be accelerated ten-fold if our countrymen were
brought to a fairer and more charitable view of the
motives of our rulers than politicians of the new
school are inclined to take, and were taught to
meet them half way in their efforts for our good.
If the newly-awakened energy of our English-
educated classes needs a sphere of activity, it will

be your duty and the duty of the Indian Patriotic Association (League, I should myself prefer to call it) to give it the proper direction, and teach it to flow in channels advantageous to themselves and to their country. There are numerous fields of patriotic usefulness yet unworked, many urgent social and economic reforms on which the energies of our youths might be profitably employed. No one need be inactive with such tasks before us as the founding of a national system of education, the introduction of moral and religious teaching into our schools, the revival of our old industries, and a host of others which a foreign Government is powerless to undertake, but in which, if we put our own shoulders honestly to the wheel, it can and will render us valuable aid.

It is well that you have taken up this noble work. Round your standard will rally true patriots of all creeds and nationalities, Indian and English Unionists, haters of the common enemies of England and India, and of the creed which has Liberty and Home Rule for its articles of faith, and Sedition and Assassination for its ritual. You will carry with you the sympathy of all ruling Princes and Chiefs, of their ministers and advisers, and of all religious bodies and orders. Our great zemindars and all the old families jealous of the honor of their race will be with you, and all those who have a stake in the country. Nor will the sinews of war be wanting to you, for few of those who join your standard but will open their purse-strings in this good cause, and if need be, lay down their lives for their country and their Queen.

Apologising for the length of this letter, and with my best respects

I remain,

MY DEAR SIR SAYED AHMED,

Yours very sincerely,

IMAD-UD-DAULAH

(SAYED HOSAIN,)

HYDERABAD, DECCAN ; }
  20th August, 1888. }

MR. MAHOMED HOSAIN HAKIM
ON
THE NATIONAL CONGRESS.

(FROM THE " PIONEER.")

A MEETING of Muhammadans was held at Bombay, at which it was decided not to send representatives to the National Congress. We quote one of the speeches made on this occasion.

Mr. Mahomed Hosain Hakim said that this year the promoters of the Congress had asked the Anjuman-i-Islam if they wished to send any of their representatives to the Congress to be held next cold weather at Allahabad. There were many who, even to this day, did not know what the Congress was really about. He was blessed by God with some common sense and knowledge, but he could not understand what possible good the movement could do to the Muhammadans, nor could he understand of what avail it would be to his Parsee and Hindu brethren. Every man of sense would admit that no rule in India had been so good, so just, and so merciful as that of the English. (Applause). The British had given them education, and would it be a reward to them for the blessing of education they had freely given to his countrymen to say— " We have now been educated enough to know how to govern our own country, and therefore we no longer want these foreigners in our midst. Let

therefore the Governor-General pack off to England,
and let the Governors of the different provinces
follow him thither.   The Civil Servants who have
come out from England must also go, and we will
rule in their stead ? "   They always professed that
they were very loyal to Government and were their
real well-wishers.   But had they reflected on what
the Congress would ultimately come to fifty or a
hundred years hence ?   Had they reflected for a
moment on its far-reaching results ?   His Hindu
and Parsee friends would pardon him for saying that
the Congress boded no good to the people, nor to
the Government either.   The organisation had
been taking a leap in the dark, little knowing where
it would land them.   (A voice : "True, quite true ").
He was sorry that some of his own community had
joined the Congress, among them being his friend the
Hon'ble Budruddin Tyabji, who was deservedly
held in the greatest esteem by every one.   Now
a son of this same gentleman had entered the Civil
Service of India, having come first in the list of the
competitors.   Would such a thing have been possible under any other Government than the British?
Had they no reason to rest contented and be thankful for what they had already got, and hope that, in
the good time to come, they might get from the
same Government more rights, as soon as they
were considered deserving of them ?   Well, then,
what was the good of their assembling in large numbers at Calcutta, Madras, or Allahabad, and joining
their voice for the intimidation of Government ?

The numbers attending these annual assemblages had been steadily increasing. Last year 600 persons attended the Congress, and a time might come when 10,000 persons might meet together. The Russians, as they were all well aware, were approaching nearer and nearer to India, and what would they think of these mighty assemblages? They would imagine that there was disunion in the enemy's camp, and that now was the time for taking advantage of it. Now, did the people wish the Russians to come and govern? They were a cruel and semi-barbarous race. They would demolish their mosques, the temples of the Hindus, and the fire-temples of the Parsees. They would grind their subjects down. Did they wish such a power to rule over them? Were not the British a thousand times better than the Russians? That being so, may the British rule of India last for evermore! (The Chairman: "*Inshallah!* May God preserve it for ever!") Look at the present political aspect of the great powers of Europe. Their relations were in a state of the utmost tension, and a spark might any day set the whole fabric in a flame. In such a state of things it was imperatively necessary for their own preservation that the races and communities of India should present a united front to their enemy; and let it be inscribed on their hearts that if they failed to make common cause against a common enemy, and continued to carry on their agitation by means of these Congresses, the consequences, fifty or a hundred years hence, might

simply prove disastrous. Then there were those who complained that Government had increased the Indian army by 10,000 men from England. But this was quite a necessary provision in view of the steady advance of the Russians in the direction of India. He would ask once again—What did Mr. Hume and others, who were interesting themselves in the Congress, want ? Did they want the country to be relieved of all the taxes ? Did they want to get rid of the police and the army ? Did they obtain no justice under the British Government ? Were they lacking in political wisdom and in capacity to govern the country wisely and well ? No. Then why would they throw away the blessing they enjoyed for the very doubtful benefits of the Congress ? It was a most difficult task to govern well a country like India. The Government had achieved wonderful success in the performance of that task, bringing peace, and security, and prosperity into the land. See what even now was the case of some of the Native States, and contrast the government there with the British rule. To this day, in Cambay, the Boree subjects were not allowed to ride on horseback. And yet some of the educated natives, instead of being thankful for what they had got, abused the Government and said that the Government were not doing this, that, and the other. With these remarks the speaker moved :—
" That it is not desirable, either from an educational point of view, or looking to the unsettled condition of Europe and Asia, even from a political

point of view, that the Muhammadan community should join the Indian National Congress in trying, however unconsciously, to force the hands of the British Government in India by an organised demonstration, however seemingly pacific in character." (Applause).

———

THE NATIONAL CONGRESS AND THE GOVERNMENT.

By Sir Syed Ahmed.

THE Hon'ble Pandit Ajudhia Nath said in the speech which he made at Lucknow in praise of the National Congress, that the Government of India approved of its objects and sympathised with it; and in proof of this he said that "the Governor-General in Calcutta and the Governor of Madras gave parties in their respective Government Houses to the members of the Congress, and invited everybody, and welcomed them warmly, and instead of raising objections, expressed their sympathy with the Congress." He further said that when an address was presented to the Governor-General he made a favourable reply, and said as much as a Viceroy of the Queen could possibly say. The Hon'ble Pandit then said "that the present was a suitable occasion for telling them that if they feared the opposition of the rulers of the North-West Provinces and Oudh, they should attach higher importance to the opinions and acts of the Governor-General and the Governor of Madras." Although I cannot believe that the favour shown by the Governor-General and the Governor of Madras to the members of the Congress was inspired by any motive other than ordinary courtesy, yet in any case I have an objection to make against these acts of the Government.

For if the Governor-General and the Governor of Madras acted thus only out of ordinary courtesy, they should at the time have taken into consideration the danger lest the people to whom they showed this kindness should make an improper use of the favour so shown. Now, however, the Government knows that the supporters of the Congress interpret this kindness in another way, and wrongfully point to the conclusions that the Governor-General and the Governor of Madras "sympathise with the objects of the Congress ;" and by this pretext try to deceive people into joining them. Government ought therefore to be very cautious in showing this kind of favour.

But if, on the other hand, the Governor-General and the Governor of Madras exhibited this favour to the members of the Congress for the reason which my friend the Hon'ble Pandit Ajudhia Nath has stated, and expressed their sympathy with the objects of the Congress, then that section of the people which is opposed to the National Congress has the gravest cause for complaint. Government knows well that there are two parties regarding the National Congress, or to be more explicit, that some nations, especially Muhammadans, are on one side, and some nations on the other. Then why should Government lean towards one side and express sympathy with it ? It is necessary for Government to hold itself aloof from both parties. Its duty is merely to stop that disturbance from which there is every reason to expect an increase of hostility between the two nations, and those acts by which general discontent is being raised against the Government. For the result of this fomentation of unreasonable discontent cannot be beneficial to the country.

I cannot imagine why my able friend the Hon'ble Pandit Ajudhia Nath should attach so much importance to the fact that Sir William Hunter, Sir Charles Turner, and three or four radical members of Parliament sympathise with the objects of the Congress. Is the government of the British Empire in their hands? Let us suppose a few members of Parliament sympathise with the National Congress, it must be remembered that there are about six hundred and fifty members in the House of Commons, leaving aside the House of Lords. Hence the significance to be attached to the support of three or four members is, as the Hindi proverb says, less than a caraway-seed in the mouth of a camel. To change the Government, or its constitution, and to substitute representative Government, is no easy matter. The people of Ireland, who have so weighty a supporter in Mr. Gladstone, besides many Members of Parliament,—what have they been able to do that our poor National Congress should think they can effect this? In my opinion if all the rulers of India should sympathise with the National Congress, yet even then the supporters of the Congress could not be successful. Some Members of Parliament may go mad, but all cannot.

Without doubt Government is itself anxious for the progress of the people of India. If the present

state of things be compared with that at the commencement of British rule, then the advancement
that the British Government has given to the people
of India is really astonishing ; and it is still inclined
in the same way to give them further advancement,
and is giving what it thinks expedient, and will
continue to give. From the uproar of the National
Congress no good result can follow. Rather it is to
be feared that those proposals for the benefit of the
people which the Government has under consideration, among which may be counted some of the
recommendations of the Public Service Commission,
may be postponed in order that the Congresswallas
may not be elated, and fancy that they have been
accomplished by their agitation. The Congress has
been in existence three years. To what Congress
do we owe the conspicuous benefits which the people
of India have received from the commencement of
the British Rule to the present day ? Similarly the
Government is ready to give further advancement
at suitable times. The Mutiny of 1857, which I
am right in calling the Sepoy War, as Mr. Kaye has
styled it, and which was due to the mistakes of some
officials, threw back the progress of India a hundred
years. If that Mutiny had not occurred, then
hundreds of our young men of a soldierly temper
would have been Volunteers ; the Arms Act would
not have been passed ; many among us would have
been Captains, and Colonels, and Generals in the
Army ; and we would have said to Government:—
" Do not trouble your European officers and British

soldiers. See—we, and we alone, will advance beyond the frontier, and will give the Russians a
practical lesson how to advance and how to give
fight."

I cannot understand the meaning of the statement of my honourable friend that people should not
fear the opposition of the rulers of the North-West
Provinces and Oudh. Whatever the opinions of
Government may be about the administration of the
country, yet it has given freedom to all its subjects
and to the newspapers to criticise its policy as they
like. Hence, if the Government of the N.-W. P.
and Oudh be opposed to the objects of the Congress,
why should those who join it fear? But, yes.
There is one thing on account of which the Congresswallas may well fear their rulers—a thing which
my honourable friend has not mentioned. Can
the Congresswallas deny—their intentions may not
be bad, and I do not charge them with bad intentions—but can they deny the fact that they have
left no stone unturned in their attempts to spread
discontent among the common people against the
Government? Are not *The Star in the East, The
Tamil Catechism* and the *Conversation between Fariduddin and Rambakhsh,* in which many statements
are false while real facts are placed in a wrong light,
as well as many other of their speeches and writings,
sufficient proof? If it be true that thousands of
copies (the Hindustani newspaper says lakhs) have
been printed in Urdu and Hindi, and circulated in
the Provinces, while the men who distribute them

say to the *banias*, " see, how oppressive the taxes
are, we are trying to remove them ;" and to suitors in
the law-courts, " see the stamp fees, what tyranny ! "
and to the landlords and cultivators, " how unjust
the revenue laws are, " and abusing Government
before every kind of man in ways appealing to his
circumstances or his comprehension ; is not this a
thing which gives the people of the N.-W. P. and
Oudh very good reason for standing in fear of their
rulers ? And is it not the duty of Government to
try to discover, by every means and method in its
power, how far this dissatisfaction has spread, and
how deep are its roots, and to ascertain whether or
not the time has come for interfering actively and
uprooting it ? Is it not the duty of Government
to prevent this disaffection from increasing, and
thus to avert a time when it would be necessary to
adopt harsh measures, such as has been done in
Ireland ? These things are included in the duty of
the Government, and Government *ought* to do
them, and it would be absurd to accuse Government
of being hostile if she were to do her duty in these
respects. The idea of my honourable friend about
the rulers of our North-West Provinces and Oudh
being opposed to the Congress, and the people
not fearing the opposition of their rulers, is absurd. In my opinion the Congresswallas need fear
nobody, but they have good reason to be afraid
of their own actions, as well as of the hostility
they are stirring up between Hindus and Muhammadans.

The Muhammadans paid no heed to the Congress for years as along as the Congresswallas told no lies about Muhammadans joining them, nor tried to secure their co-operation by deceitful methods.   But in the Madras Congress they began to adopt this procedure, and to try to induce Muhammadans to take a part.   Then those Muhammadans who wished to protect their nation from the bad results of the Congress stood up and warned their people of its evil effects.

SYED AHMED.

THE "PIONEER" ON SEDITION.

THE two following leaders have appeared in the *Pioneer*, the leading English journal in India, on the seditious methods adopted by the National Congress :—

The Spread of Sedition.

With characteristic indifference we are taking no steps to deal with the latest and most dangerous development of popular agitation in India. The Congress *Catechism* and its other incendiary tracts are being distributed every day in larger numbers in the vernaculars of India. In the Punjab the ground is "being prepared" by this means for the Congress of December, 1889. In Guzerat the agitators boast of having printed 35,000 copies in the local vernacular. The leading ideas of the *Catechism* are utterly subversive of British rule. First, it is assumed throughout that the present condition of the country is miserable. Frequent allusion is made to "our many grievances" and to "our hardships and disadvantages." Next, the people are told that they can expect no assistance either from Anglo-Indian officials, who "wish to keep matters as they are," or from the Indian Government. It is clear that this idea cuts at the root of loyalty, while it presents the rulers of the country in the light of tyrants. To remedy this state of things the prospect is held out of coercing the Indian Government by means of English public opinion.

Such a state of things, if possible, would mean ruin
to the prestige of the Government and to its
strength.   Finally, the object towards which this
coercion is to be directed is that "a Parliament
must be established" in India.   Mr. Hume confess-
ed that this idiotic dream was his goal, but he
generously allowed fifty or seventy years for its
realisation.   The *Catechism* points exultingly to
the glorious time after "a year or two when we
have won the day."   Thus these four main ideas of
the *Catechism* inculcate discontent, antagonism to
the rulers, contempt for their authority, and revolution.   This propaganda is dignified with the name
of the "political education of the masses."   To
suppose that it will have no effect is to argue
sheer ignorance of the people of Upper India.
We have heard of a case of one of these pamphlets being read out before a crowd of ignorant
men of a fighting caste, the result being that they
became very excited, and cried out—"God grant
that the fighting comes soon."   The pamphlets had
been distributed by a Bengali.   To add to the
effect of this seditious literature, the agitators are
themselves travelling up and down the land abusing the Government and conjuring up chimerical
visions of prosperity if the people do but unite and
insist in having representative government.   No
argument is too absurd if a few ignorant supporters
can by its means be gained.   A Musalman named
Bhimji has been touring over the Provinces and
telling the Muhammadans that if they joined the

National Congress their holy cities—Mecca, Meshed, and Jerusalem—would be better protected. Fancy, a Bengali garrison defending Mecca against the attacks of the infidels! He further drew attention to the poverty of the poor, and said that all this would be removed if the National Congress had its way. While this is going on in the vernacular the Anglo-Bengali Press from Calcutta to Lahore, with one or two exceptions, is attacking the Viceroy, the Government, and Anglo-Indians at large with a virulence that can only be explained as the result of malice united to the belief that Government is cowardly in the face of abuse. To embitter race-feeling the *Tribune*, a Bengali paper of Lahore, has even assailed the modesty and chastity of English ladies. Every scandal, true or false, that can be gleaned from the four corners of the Empire, is greedily laid hold of and served up to feed the appetites of the detractors of British rule. The result is, that throughout the English-reading Hindu public a settled discontent is spreading, based on misconceptions and untruths. Again, our easy-going nature thinks that truth will prevail in the end. But we forget that the Mutiny of 1857 was due to a misconception, namely, that the Government was planning an attack on the religions of the people. Government has been solemnly warned of the danger of letting this state of things continue by men who know the people far better than we do. Natives of India, among the most able, influential and honourable in the land—Sir Syed Ahmed, Mr. Syed Hosain

Bilgrami, the Maharaja of Benares, Sir Salar Jung, the Raja of Binga, Munshi Imtiaz Ali, and many others—have stated their firm conviction that if this agitation proceeds long enough, it will lead to a terrible catastrophe. Now, what has been the attitude of Government towards this rival and extraordinary propaganda? The *Catechism* undertakes to answer this question. It says that the Finance Commission and the Public Service Commission were the direct results of the Congress ; and it goes on to state that Mr. Gladstone and Mr. Chamberlain have declared themselves in its favour. The Congresswallas make great capital out of the circumstance that they were invited to the Government Houses in Calcutta and Madras: this fact being triumphantly paraded before the people in every oration as conclusive proof that Government approves of their agitation. The Hon'ble Pandit Ajudhia Nath said, in his speech at Lucknow, that " the Governor-General in Calcutta and the Governor in Madras gave parties to the members of the Congress in their respective Government Houses, and called them all and received them kindly, and instead of making objections, expressed their sympathy with the aims of the Congress." But unfortunately the Congress- wallas need not rely entirely on misrepresentation in their attempts to prove Government to be on their side. The strong advocacy of their cause by Sir W. Hunter, a man on whom the Government had lavished its honours, is, in the absence of any rejoinder, a conspicuous victory, and has given a very great

stimulus to the movement.   The active support of
Mr. Hume and several unofficial Europeans is an
indication of support from people closely connected
with the rulers.   They have further had the wit to
secure a prominent Englishman of Calcutta as their
next President.   And, finally, the Congress has
achieved a triumph in the pronounced approval of its
methods by the Governor of Bombay.   Lord Reay
must welcome, he says, anything that tends to improve the administration.   One of the improvements
suggested by the Congresswallas, with that singular
want of political insight which prevents them from
seeing even their own interests, was the abolition
of the Governorships of Madras and Bombay.   Perhaps when the Governor of Bombay has been improved out of existence, His Excellency may have
time to reflect on the inadvisability of playing at
fireworks in a powder magazine.

It would appear, therefore, that the Congress
agitators can lay claim to some social countenance
and a certain amount of support in high quarters,
which they do their utmost to magnify in the eyes of
the uninformed public: and that the Supreme Government has contented itself with a mysterious silence,
while its very existence is being undermined, and
aspirations are being encouraged in the people which,
being preposterous and unrealisable, are doomed to
bitter disappointment.   What is the cause of so ano-
malous a state of things ?   The cause is to be found
in the singular elasticity of the proposals of the
Congress.   To the English public it shows itself, as

an English member of Parliament remarked, "ridi-
culously moderate" in its demands.   It merely wants
certain changes tending "to improve the administration," while the solid groundwork itself is to remain
untouched.   But to the ignorant masses it presents
a very different front.   It knows it can catch their
allegiance by no such mild proposals.   Nothing less
than the abolition of taxation and the expulsion of
the hated foreigner are the baits held out to popular
ignorance and fanaticism.   English supporters of
the movement imagine that these are mere excres-
cences that will disappear in time.   They are, on
the contrary, the vital principles of the movement,
and the apparent moderation of its formal demands
is simply a diplomatic device in order to gain a van-
tage ground from the enemy for a further advance.
The originators of the Congress showed their wisdom in assuming that we fall easy dupes to a little
palaver.   A little anecdote may here be mentioned.
Two Englishmen, accompanied by a native friend,
were walking one evening in an Indian town.   One
of them was a visitor from England ; the other had
recently come to the country.   They were accosted
by a jovial, English-speaking Hindu, who joined
himself to the party, offered them his carriage, and
escorted them to their hotel, holding forth magni-
ficently on the depths of his loyalty, and how nothing
could give him greater pleasure than to die for his
Queen.   Having arrived at the hotel he called for
a peg, and remarked to the native member of the
trio that he knew well how to catch the owls.   So

it is with Mr. Hume and the Congresswallas. Unfortunately they, too, know how to catch the owls.

Such being then the attitude of the Congress towards the Government and the attitude of the Government towards the Congress, the question that arises before anyone who does not wish to see the mischief grow, is whether there is no means open of allaying or averting it. But to consider this it is necessary to take into account the feelings of that not inconsiderable portion of the population which is either outside the pale of the agitation or actively opposed to it: and this involves an extended train of argument which must be reserved for a separate article.

Sedition and its Antidote.

After treating of the character of the propaganda that is being spread throughout the country by the working party of the National Congress, we were brought up at the question—How Government is to deal with this fever that has seized on the body politic ? The simple and straightforward method would be direct suppression, for which purpose a dozen policemen would be ample. But it is doubtful whether the British public would tolerate interference with the Press and the right of public meeting before the bloodshed came to enlighten its wits. And when the bloodshed comes, whether between Hindu and Muhammadan, or between Englishman and sepoy, the flame may spread so fast as to make its extinction very difficult, especially if synchronous with a Russian war. However, without applying to England for a Coercion Act like that in force in Ireland, there appear to be ways in which the Government of India could vastly diminish the evil.

In Upper India there are three communities to be dealt with. First, the Bengalis, who are settled or employed in large numbers in the Provinces. They are the backbone of the Congress movement. In dealing with them no arguments are of any avail. Lord Dufferin personally appealed to them to moderate the tone of their Press. The consequence was, they redoubled their vituperation. This is the result of treating them as gentlemen, amenable to reason. They have one unanswerable reply, that their method pays. They are intoxicated with success. However, deeds and not words would very soon produce an astonishing change in their convictions. The second community are the up-country Hindus. At present they are undecided. Some, including their noblest caste, the Rajputs, are against the Congress; some are in its favour; and many are wavering, not knowing whether or not to accept the Bengalis, whom they dislike, as their leaders. It remains for Government, by throwing its weight in the scale, either to preserve the loyalty of the up-country Hindus, or to turn them as a nation into a seditious band far more dangerous than the Bengalis. The third community are the Muhammadans. These detest the Congress cordially, as the triumph of democratic principles means for them utter and hopeless ruin. They are like the men of Ulster in Ireland without their wealth and education. But in dealing with the Muhammadans two great facts should be borne in mind. First, there is an almost universal and intense longing for reconciliation with their old foes, for friendship with their rulers. Their long series of misfortunes has crushed the old spirit of rivalry, and it needs but a slight manifestation of friendship to win their devoted loyalty. The second fact is their ignorance how to effect this reconciliation. They behave according to their traditional method and refuse to embarrass the Government. They see the country overrun by Bengalis, who publicly and privately do nothing but abuse the Government. Hence they sometimes argue that the way to please their eccentric rulers appears to be by abusing them. And there is a real and serious danger of old-fashioned Muhammadans imagining, from the extraordinary attitude preserved by Government in this Congress agitation, that it is really in favour of the Congress. A clear indication of this danger may be seen in the report of some Congress meetings held in Ludhiana. The itinerant lecturer Bhimji managed to convert an old Maulvi, who made a speech in the Jumma Musjid, in which he said that " the National Congress was a blessing sent by God for the relief of millions of poor people who at the present time were starving." Various remarks in the report clearly indicate that Bhimji had managed to produce an impression that Government was for the Congress, and that without this impression he could not have secured the support of this influential but uninformed Maulvi.   The opponents of the Congress were stigmatised as Wahabis and enemies of British rule ; and it was said that Bhimji called on the Deputy Commissioner and the District Judge, " both of whom received him most kindly, and expressed their sympathy in his public-spirited mission."   It was further stated that the police were used to disperse an anti-Congress meeting and to protect a Congress meeting.   It is obvious, therefore, that the adoption by Government of a negative policy, relying on the two parties to fight it out, is an unsafe one.   In the first place, it is capable of misinterpretation.   In the second place, in a fight between two popular parties, in which one side promises everything and the other side nothing, what chance is there of victory for the latter?   And again, what guarantee is there that even the agitation that has sprung up against the Congress may not in the future take a dangerous course ?

Things have, in fact, come to a pass when it is well for Government to review the principles on which India has been governed, for there are indications that it is fast becoming a second Ireland. We are threatened not only with " National " Congresses, but with perpetual Provincial Congresses in every part of India.   The agitation is growing by leaps and bounds.   The present condition of the Bengali community should be a solemn warning as to where our methods are leading us.   We have given them more favours than we can possibly give to any

other race in India, because not only did we find
them at a lower level, but we have put them to rule
in many countries in which they are foreigners;
and yet they are ostentatiously disloyal, as no other
people in India are.

What is the cause of this? Not so much perhaps education, as some imagine; but the whole
policy and principles of our rule which foster
methods that run into sedition, and do nothing to
encourage loyalty. Loyalty should be the watch-
word of our policy. Loyalty, carefully tested, should
be the supreme virtue recognised by Government.
Men should be given high posts only if their loyalty
be proved; and, if well proved, loyalty should be
rewarded much more liberally than has hitherto been
the case. Loyalty to the Government whose salt
one has tasted was the most sacred of Oriental
political virtues. It was the pivot of Eastern States.
At present it holds in the Native Army, but it is fast
disappearing in "New India." If a man give proof
of loyalty he is blackguarded by every Bengali paper
as a sycophant and a flatterer, but if he abuse
Government, they laud him as a man of public spirit
and of independence. In a dozen ways we ourselves
encourage this. When a man is troublesome we
reward him with a high post to induce him to keep
his mouth shut (which he seldom does), and so
produce fifty imitators. When we give favours we
manage to do it in such a way as to inspire no
gratitude. We give it not as a favour but as a
right, or we even admit it as a claim. We let it

appear not as if we had given it but as if it had been taken from us. The policy of Akbar was to crush opposition, and then, when his enemies felt wholly powerless and at his mercy, to raise them up and shower on them his favours. In this way he won their devoted loyalty. Loyalty of the heart and feelings of personal gratitude to Government—sentiments strong under Muhammadan rule, but weak under ours—have to be carefully fostered. In England they are unnecessary. But Government in India is on far weaker basis than Government in England. The Government is foreign and painful to sentiments of national honour. The disgusting manner of the increasing numbers of low class Europeans and Eurasians towards natives of rank is a source of constantly growing friction. There must be created feelings of personal loyalty to counteract this. But one essential element in this sentiment is a feeling of respect and awe. This can never exist if the rulers appear weak, timid, and frightened of their subjects. Their prestige and their unquestioned power must be maintained. But here a common English misconception must be removed. The prestige of Government rests on the prestige and position of those persons only who are by virtue of their position rulers, not on the prestige of every Englishman as member of a ruling race. The latter idea is odious to the people. It encourages every Englishman of the lower orders to swagger as if he were the Viceroy. We should show ourselves as jealous of the honour and position of natives of rank as of our own. In testing loyalty the first criterion is that a man's acts and words should tend to make people at large contented. To stir up discontent should be treason. Methods of attacking Government, which have the least tendency to run into sedition, should be suppressed with a firm hand. Englishmen have a natural tendency to sympathise with any kind of healthy activity which appears among the people. But the safety of the Empire demands that this activity, whether English or native, should be confined within narrower bounds than are permissible in England. If people—Englishmen no less than natives—overstep these bounds they must be taught their mistake. The National Congress has overstepped these bounds. Its strength or its weakness now depends entirely on ourselves. If it be seen that proposals for the advancement of the people suffer rather than gain by being debated in the Congress, the Congress will very soon collapse like a soap-bubble. But if our statesmen stand with hands joined before a spurious public opinion, always giving in a little to popular clamour, the time is possibly not far distant when they will have to make way for the men of iron with the Commander-in-Chief at their head.

THE COMING MUTINY IN INDIA.

By Choudhri Nasrat Ali.

THE notorious pamphlet published in English and Urdu and purporting to be a conversation between two fictitious persons, Maulvi Fariduddin and Rambakhsh, gives some idea of the emphatically disloyal sentiments entertained by the founder of the National Congress and his co-adjutors, who, by constantly fanning the flame of rebellion, are trying to produce a general conflagration which will envelope the whole of India, and which it will be difficult to suppress or extinguish. They are foolishly endeavouring to conceal the fire beneath the ashes which has at last smoked out in and through the pamphlet. Beneath the ashes lie smouldering, not little sparks which might die out by themselves, but gigantic blocks of wood which will blaze out and destroy the public peace.

Every intelligent man, who cares to read the pamphlet, will be driven to the conclusion that a wide dissemination of such disloyal and revolutionary notions will one day make the well-contented and peaceful citizens, who clearly see danger in the present agitation, and who do not like the peace of the country to be disturbed and the social fabric to be destroyed by the flames of rebellion, forget the disastrous events of 1857.

The pamphlet was first published in English, but in order to secure universal circulation among the masses, it was subsequently translated into *Urdu*, and many thousand copies of the Urdu version have been distributed gratis in Lucknow and the neighbouring towns and villages.

Mr. Hume and the partizans of the Congress have made many frivolous pretexts, and put forth pleas which are altogether inadmissible. The distribution of many thousand Urdu copies of a distinctly seditious publication must be taken to indicate a desire to throw the country into a political ferment, and create rebellion. This is clearly stated in the pamphlet itself to be its aim and object. The revised pamphlet was re-published in 1887, and incorporated with the report of the Madras National Congress. Greatly annoyed and distressed at Mr. Theodore Beck's sharp review of the pamphlet,* wherein he has called the serious attention of the Government to the distinctly seditious character of the publication, Mr. Hume has set up a weak defence and denied all responsibility for it. He has further insisted that controversial articles which were published three or four years ago should not be called in question now. This is not a satisfactory reply, for it was under Mr. Hume's personal responsibility and immediate control as General Secretary to the Congress, that the report for 1887 has been printed and published with the objectionable pamphlet full of seditious notions, as an appendix.

People are astonished at the extreme violence of the Congress and the Anti-Congress demonstrations

---

* The pamphlet here alluded to is *The Star in the East.*—ED.

lately witnessed at Lucknow and in its vicinity. The Congressists ascribe this to the strong Anti-Congress feelings excited by the political lecture delivered by the Hon'ble Sir Syed Ahmed Khan at Lucknow, on the 27th December, 1887.   This is utterly wrong, and is intended to mislead those not acquainted with the real state of things.   The violence of the Anti-Congress demonstration was owing, as a matter of fact, to the wide distribution in Lucknow and its neighbourhood of many thousand copies of the seditious pamphlet, wherein the British Government is strongly condemned as a grinding despotism, and the people are called upon to rebel against it.   Those who desire peace at any cost and who know by experience how the mutiny, only thirty years ago, spread like wild fire among the ignorant and brave races of Upper India, and what disastrous results it produced, clearly perceived the danger and determined to oppose the Congress, which is its real source, and stem the tide of mutiny before it had attained the magnitude and strength of a disastrous flood.

The people of Lower Bengal cannot realize the real character of the Mutiny of 1857 and the calamities and hardships it brought in its train.   European gentlemen and their families were cruelly murdered by the brutal native soldiery as if they were born to be butchered or tortured to death. Thousands of natives who were suspected of being in " touch " with the British or of possessing wealth, were plundered and murdered in cold blood.   At

Amethi, a respectable native gentleman was most cruelly tortured to death by the rebels, who poured gunpowder into his ears and mouth and then set it on fire, blowing away the poor man's brains simply because they mistook him for a wealthy man, and demanded of him a large sum which he could not pay. People were plundered to an unlimited extent. A plunderer went about the country with two bullocks loaded with ornaments plundered from Hindu and Muhammadan women.

The disastrous events of 1857 are remembered to this day with deep horror. Thousands of respectable women threw themselves into wells, tanks, and rivers, preferring death to dishonor. The atrocities perpetrated by the Russian soldiery on the Musalman population of Bulgaria after the Russo-Turkish war of 1877, resemble in character and extent those perpetrated by the brutal rebels upon Englishmen and natives in 1857.

The object of the writers, the printers, and the publishers of this seditious pamphlet seems to be to re-kindle the flame of rebellion throughout British India, which, in 1857, touched only a portion of Upper India. Like flint they have sparks concealed within them and are seeking for an opportunity to let the hidden fire blaze out. Had they not been actuated by sinister motives, they would have confined their teachings to the intelligent and the cultured, and would not have circulated all this seditious stuff among the reckless, whose rashness makes them long for the sword which has

been taken away from them to ensure peace and
tranquillity. If the ignorant masses are re-armed,
then I confidently assert that they will not be able
to distinguish between a lawful and an unlawful use
of their weapons, for they still retain their primitive
rashness, and can only tear the Indian Penal Code
to pieces and twist the torn leaves into small bundles
of grocery. It is a grave apprehension of such
danger that has compelled the Musalmans of India
as a whole, and many respectable and influential
Hindus, to endeavour most strenuously to check
the growing evil and prevent the coming storm.

Nothing can be more convincing than the evidence afforded by the fact that the British Indian
Association of Oudh, considering the Congress
movement distinctly seditious, convened a General
Meeting on the 4th April, 1888, at which a Resolution was unanimously passed disclaiming all connection therewith. This is a political Association of
the Maharajas, the Rajas, and the Talukdars of
Oudh, both Hindus and Musalmans, and I have
the honor of being the Assistant Secretary to this
important Association. I say that the Talukdars'
Association has rightly sounded the note of alarm,
clearly perceiving the seditious forces which the
founder and the promoters of the Congress are
setting in motion. It was in no uncertain tones
that an influential member of the Association, an
Hon'ble Maharaja, spoke of the Congress as
foreboding the disastrous events of 1857. It is
therefore utterly wrong to say that it is Mr. Beck

only who has taken an alarmist view of the Congress agitation, as a similar opinion was publicly expressed by a great Talukdar of Oudh some time before Mr. Beck's trenchant articles appeared in public print. Do not the partizans of the Congress remember the remark made by a German to Nawab Fateh Nawaz Jung of Hyderabad while travelling in Europe, that the people of India had conspired against the British Government? Such being the general impression produced by the action of the Congress in foreign countries, which can know anything about India through newspapers only, great must be the danger apprehended by the peaceful inhabitants of this country from the practical measures adopted and carried out by the Congresswallas with such *éclat*. If such seditious ideas continue to be promulgated, the evil day may not be far distant when the whole country will be drenched in blood like the clothes of the Hindus besmeared with the conventional red powder during the Holi festival.

Before this notorious pamphlet had been printed and published as part and parcel of the Congress Report for 1887, on the direct responsibility of the Congress, the responsibility of publishing it in English rested with a few persons only ; while the person or persons who had published an Urdu version of it might have alleged that they were responsible only for what was, after all, a translation, though this plea looks like holding up one's hand to save one's head from being struck off with the sword. But from the fact of the objectionable pamphlet being incorporated with the Annual Report of the Congress, not Mr. Hume only, but every member and supporter of the movement, has become answerable for its disloyal ideas and tone. God only knows what made the Congressists incorporate this seditious pamphlet with the printed record of their proceedings, and how the man who has published it has escaped the punishment prescribed by law.

The foregoing remarks, far from being merely sentimental, are the result of my personal observation. They may appear very strange to those not acquainted with the real state of things, or who have not had the opportunity of seeing with their own eyes the mutinous spirit and the seditious proceedings of the Congressists. But with the overwhelming evidence before us there ought to be no doubt or misapprehension.

In support of what I have said above, I may refer the reader to those passages in the pamphlet which are calculated to arouse the general popular feelings against the British Government. I say it is advisable to check the disease before it gets firm hold of the system. Snake-bite is at first confined to a tip-toe, but when the poison pervades the whole system, no remedy can be applied with effect.

The pamphlet consists of a conversation between two fictitious persons, Maulvi Fariduddin and Rambakhsh, the former a pleader of a district called Hakikatabad, and the latter the mukaddam or

headman of the village Kambakhtpur. The political condition of Kambakhtpur, which means literally an unlucky village, is vividly contrasted with
that of Shamshpur, another and a remarkably pros-
perous village. The former is represented as being
under the despotic rule of one Raja Harbans Rai,
and the latter as being under the constitutional government of another Raja named Dharam Singh.
The one implies the despotism of the Indian Government and the other the constitutional government
of England. Maulvi Fariduddin is represented as
persuading Rambakhsh into the belief that if he
wished to be relieved from the tyranny of a despotic
Government, he must seek for a representative one,
and co-operate with his educated and wealthy countrymen for obtaining the desired change ; and that
if he did this, the English nation would compel the
Government to comply with the wishes of the educated natives. From beginning to end the pamphlet is an uniform and persistent attempt to show that
the Government of India is an oppressive despotism, and that it is the duty of the native population
to oppose their oppressors, might and main. Ignorant people are deluded into the belief that the
people of the United Kingdom (meaning perhaps
the Irish malcontents) will support their pretensions.
Some professed organs of the Congress party have
at last broken the spell, and plainly suggested that
the Congresswallas ought to adopt the tactics of
the Irish Home Rulers and raise funds. Great
stress is laid on the views of Sir William Hunter,

and it is said that the learned Doctor being a confidential adviser of the Government, his letters in the *Times* truly reflect the decision of Her Majesty's Government.   The reason generally assigned for this decision is that the British Government, fully conscious of its own weakness and inability to oppose Russia, contemplates making over the country to the natives.   I have myself heard an educated native talking such nonsense to one of his temper and tastes amid the jeers and laughter of his jolly companions.   A series of articles in the London *Times* are fondly regarded as an unmistakable sign of victory ; and with the leading English journal coming forward to support the cause of the Congress, representative institutions for India are, with these radical faddists, a foregone conclusion and an accomplished fact.

They foolishly depend for success in the attainment of their object upon those who are the component parts or consistent elements of British Government.   These are honest men, no doubt, but not fools.   Perhaps they do not sufficiently realize the fact that the population of India consists of an almost endless variety of nations, tribes, and sects, diametrically opposed to each other in their religious creeds, their social institutions, and their political interests.   Geographically, India is but a peninsula, but from the vastness and heterogeneousness of her population she looks like a great continent.   The inhabitants of one part of the country materially differ from those inhabiting the other, not only in religion but in language, manners, and customs, and all the essential elements of social life.   They do not at all seem to be the natives of one and the same country.   Among Asiatic nations, religion occupies the foremost place in all their thoughts and actions.   It serves as a touchstone for testing every problem, moral, social, or political.   The native population chiefly consists of Hindus and Musalmans, who stand in the ratio of 5 to 1.   Numerically, the other nations are extremely insignificant.   How a well-balanced representative Government or Council is possible in a country so circumstanced, passes human comprehension ; and if the balance of power cannot possibly be preserved between the rival sects and races, the inevitable majority of one in the Legislative Councils constituted on a representative basis, will naturally be strongly resented by the other.   It would be utterly impossible to reconcile conflicting interests in such a Council.   " It is puerile," rightly observed the Hon'ble Sir Syed Ahmed Khan in his famous political lecture, " to talk of two hostile races fighting with each other most fanatically outside the Council-room, and maintaining perfect good-will and concord between themselves inside the Legislative Chamber." *   Not only the Muhammadans as a whole, but many respectable and influential Hindus also have come to regard the spread of sedition through the Congress as extremely dangerous to the peace of the country.   Fully convinced of the utter

---

* This was said by Sir Syed Ahmed in a letter to the *Pioneer*.

impracticability of representative institutions in a country like India, they naturally look upon those who are longing for them as "building castles in the air." Those who apprehend serious danger to their country and their society, not only from the seditious pamphlet, but from the inflammatory speeches and underhanded proceedings of the Congressists, are naturally anxious to see the mischievous agitation summarily put down. The British Government has been mildly but deliberately overlooking these seditious proceedings, but it must be remembered that these same proceedings will one day compel it to take action.

As representative institutions, as demanded by the Congressists, cannot be worked in a country like India, the question naturally arises—In what will the spread of sedition end ? The answer to this is obvious. It must end either in setting the ignorant masses, whose loyalty is thus being undermined, against the Government, and thus involving the Government and the loyalist party in trouble, or in the discomfiture of the party of sedition-mongers. In either case, the peace of the country is seriously compromised.

The partizans of the Congress will object to the use of the word *loyalist* in the above sentence ; but they must understand that our loyalty is not due to " white men " as such, but to their beneficent rule under which we enjoy the inestimable blessings of peace and civilisation. I know full well that my outspokenness exposes me to sharp personal attacks;

but as a sincere Musalman and a representative of my community, I declare that the Musalmans are bound by their religion not to excite sedition and foment rebellion against their rulers for the time being. If they do this, they are sinners in the eye of God, and if they die in the state of rebellion, they will not enjoy that eternal bliss in Paradise, which they have so much coveted through their lives.

I am glad to find that my right-thinking and far-sighted Hindu countrymen are as much bent on stamping out sedition as I am, for they as well as I fully realize the fact that the attempt to set up a representative government in India is both senseless and hopeless, like the effort of a baby to catch hold of the moon by stretching out its little arms in the belief that it will successfully accomplish the feat.

The pamphlet represents the Viceroy of India as an unscrupulous Raja, and the English officers as reckless *Hakims* or tyrants, loth to hear and re-dress the grievances of their subjects, who are thus forced to regard their chief ruler (the Viceroy) as politically dead. They are further taught to believe that they are being ground down by their despotic rulers in a thousand ways. Rent is extorted from them before the proper time, no allowance is made for a bad harvest, and even their ploughs and bullocks are sold. No doubt these false charges have been brought against the Government with the object of turning a loyal and contented people into disloyal and discontented subjects. Such grievances, if they are really found and felt anywhere, may be represented through a free Press, and equally free public associations, which already exist in large numbers. This safe and effective plan for ventilating popular grievances, real or imaginary, was rightly suggested by the Oudh Talukdars' Association, but it did not find favor with those who prefer dodging and skulking to plain sailing. The Government is calumniated and denounced before an ignorant and excitable populace which cannot understand the current political problems, cannot realize the administrative difficulties which surround their rulers, and cannot judge of the soundness or otherwise of the policy which the Government ought to pursue with due regard to existing circumstances and conditions.

To spread sedition in the country, the pamphlet has been translated into colloquial Urdu, easily intelligible to rude peasants and ignorant villagers steeped in their primitive barbarism.

The writer of the pamphlet seems to be an average man with a modicum of common sense and with very hazy notions of the subject he is treating of. While deliberately exposing the dark side of the picture, he has carefully concealed the bright side of it. He ought to have asked some zemindar whether the Government does not postpone the realization of the revenue for a bad harvest; whether it does not sanction remissions for crops injured or destroyed by hail; whether it has not exempted by law agricultural implements from distraint and sale even in execution of a decree.

Furthermore, the pamphlet plainly says that the British Government is despotic both in its constitution and its actions, that the Queen-Empress, who has never visited India, has made over this unfortunate country to the Viceroy and his subordinate officers, who, like Raja Harbans Rai of Kambakhtpur, are unscrupulous tryants, who are squandering away millions of rupees extorted from the poor people, and who are by their oppressive rule creating strong discontent in the country. Who that knows the people can say that such notions are not calculated to poison their hearts against their rulers? Can the people at large understand the Budget account? If not, they are at least being taught to treat their English rulers as their enemies who are working their ruin, and upon whom it will be their duty, as true children of the soil, to avenge their wrongs when the day of retribution comes.

Further on, it is plainly stated that the present being a despotic Government, should no longer be suffered to exist. But here the fault is attributed to the system rather than to the officers of Government, who are said to be bound to respect the existing depotism equally with the subject-races.

The writer of the pamphlet seems to have a short memory. In the first few pages he has represented the *gomashtas* or local officers as utterly careless of their charge, but further on he has painted the

English Collector in the most hideous colours, and tried to make of him a " Nero " in miniature. Of this I shall write more fully hereafter.

I do not know by what means it is sought to get rid of the present Government. That at the last meeting of the Congress Babu Surendranath Banerji strongly insisted on the Indian Arms Act being repealed forthwith, furnishes a clue to the motives at work.

The British Government may be for or against the introduction of representative institutions in this country ; but I would respectfully remind the Government that the manlier races of Upper India, apprehensive of serious mischief to themselves as a nation or nations, are fully prepared to oppose the so-called reform, might and main. Nature has so arranged the different nations making up the population of India that the weaker nation cannot reasonably expect justice and fair play from the stronger one. I confess I cannot pin my faith on a single newspaper letter from Mr. Budruddin Tyabji promising fair play to all who would enter the Congress and join in the senseless cry for representative institutions ; nor can I trust even a solemn pledge to smooth down numerical and other inequalities between rival races, contending parties, and opposite sects, whose representatives are to be the future rulers of the country. I cannot really believe that in the Council Chamber the law of the majority will not prevail, and that the party which has the largest number of supporters in the country will not command a working majority in the Council. Such a pledge is transient and shadowy, like a dust-storm which rises up only to vanish in the thin air.

"The pamphlet" endeavours to excite the hatred of that "terrible swarm of locusts," i. e., the great mass of ignorant cultivators and rude villagers against the British Government, by telling them that they are being ruined by enhanced rent and increased taxation on land. Of course, the object aimed at is to make them hate the Government as a cruel despotism ; and extremely foolish as they are, it is easy to make them believe such foolish things. Being myself a zemindar of Oudh, I know very well that the landholders of the province possessed unlimited powers to enhance their rents prior to the passing of Act XX of 1886, and that many well-to-do cultivators who had acquired land by purchase became zemindars and enhanced the rents of their estates. I do not mean to say that they practised extortions upon their tenants and squeezed more money out of them than was justified by the capacities of their holdings or the necessities of management. Rents were enhanced in proportion to the rise in the value of land, increased facilities for cultivation, and increased produce of land. Cultivators were never deprived of their proper share of the improvements effected by human ingenuity, and it was to these improvements that the rapid rise in the value of land and a proportionate enhancement of rent were mainly due. The writer of the pamphlet, if he were an honest and candid man, would have attributed the poverty of the cultivators to the systematic exactions of the *Mahajan* or village banker, but this he would not do and has not done, his real object being to show that the Government and its officers are abominable despots. Perhaps he was not aware of the fact that by Act XX of 1886, the Government has reduced to a minimum the practically unlimited powers of enhancement of rent previously exercised by zemindars, who can now under the new law enhance their rents only once after every seven years, and even then at the moderate rate of one anna per rupee or 6-4 per cent. The wonder is that the Government has been severely blamed, instead of being warmly praised, for all it has done for the great body of cultivators.

Further on, the pamphlet plainly says that the present being a despotic Government has been working the country's ruin, and as a natural consequence, must be got rid of at all costs. Well and bravely said! This fearless outspokenness on the part of the indomitable writer of the pamphlet might fairly be rewarded with the exalted rank of the Commander-in-Chief of the rebellious forces in the coming mutiny. Of course, the Congresswallas would jump to the conclusion that representative institutions are only the panacea for the evil, but to the sober judgment of all sound and candid observers, representative institutions are utterly impracticable in a country like India, split up as it is by a thousand and one differences and dissensions.

To show that the present is a purely despotic Government and that its officers are tyrants, a sensational story is concocted about an English Collector, who is painted in hideous colours as a petty tyrant, and Rambakhsh is represented as telling Maulvi Fariduddin how cruelly he (Rambakhsh) was whipped 30 years ago by order of this English Collector, and how ashamed he felt of showing the lower part of his body, which still bore the marks of the stripes.   The latter part of the above sentence is a pure fiction, as, in fact, is the whole story ; and it is unquestionably meant to excite the people against the Government, for the *dhoti* commonly worn by the Indian peasant very imperfectly covers the lower part of his body.   The writer of the pamphlet would have acted more wisely and to some purpose if, before preaching war against the Government, he had introduced a much-needed reform in the ordinary dress of the rude peasant of Upper India, or even in the wearing apparel of the more civilized inhabitants of Lower Bengal, where the notorious *sari*, a thin and flimsy piece of cloth, generally prevails.

The story, as related by Rambakhsh, runs thus :—" Once it so happened that the brutal English Collector came to inspect the village where I reside. The usual supply of grass for the Collector's camp was somehow delayed.   The Tehsildar, Murtaza Shah, a notoriously bad character, who had once been convicted of forcible extortion and punished by transportation, pleaded his innocence before the

incensed Collector and laid the blame at my door.
The heartless tyrant caused me to be cruelly whipped, called me a 'pig' and a 'block-head,' and threatened me with ruin, saying he would teach me how
to obey the *Hakim*.   He again ordered his *khallasi*
to inflict thirty stripes on the lower part of my body,
so I was bound, hand and foot, and whipped most
severely, till I fell senseless on the ground."

Comment on the above is unnecessary.   Is not
this an outrage upon truth and common sense?
The writer of the pamphlet fears neither God nor
man, and most audaciously sets the Government
at defiance.   Even the native Tehsildar has been
incriminated and stigmatized as a petty tyrant
simply because he was an officer of a despotic
Government!

Such a startling incident, I say, has never
occurred since the establishment of British rule in
this country, for who has ever heard of a district
officer holding a villager punishable under the Penal
Code for failure to supply grass, and causing him to
be whipped almost to death?   No doubt such sensational stories are invented with the criminal intent
to undermine the loyalty of the rude peasantry who
are completely swayed by their brutal instincts, and
are scarcely amenable to reason.   The pamphlet
starts upon the idea that sedition is of little or no
effect, unless it spreads among the ignorant and
brave people.   I hope the Government will pardon
me if I should call its reticence, impolitic and inexpedient.   That it is a harmless beginning of the

end I quite admit; but I would point out that a
house is not burnt to ashes the moment it is set on
fire. Radicalism has become more powerful in
India than Nihilism in Russia, for while the Russian
Nihilists seek to destroy the existing Government
by secret machinations, the Indian Radicals openly
and fearlessly denounce the Indian Government as
the worst type of despotism, and are strenuously endeavouring, by inventing and publishing false stories,
to make every member of the subject-race a pronounced enemy of the Government. I am really
astonished at the foolish credulity of my countrymen,
who seem to think it a child's play to pull off the mou-
stache of the living lion! I wish they could realize
the fact that such deliberate misrepresentations
reflect seriously upon their truthfulness and loyalty.
They seem to have taken it for granted that the
British Government is blind of both eyes and that
its officers are simply fools. The Congresswallas
seem to believe that an unarmed populace would be
able by mere brute force to shake the Government
to its foundation, just as a violent earthquake once
convulsed the land of Kashmir, and would even-
tually pull down the tottering building and construct
a new and a more durable one with Bengalis for its
main pillars.

They also foolishly imagine that the people of
England would readily believe what they have
never seen with their own eyes. This is the reason
assigned by Mr. Hume in his reply to Mr. Beck
for publishing such seditious writings.

Further on, the pamphlet says that the brutal Collector was compelled by the Government to resign, and would have been dismissed but for the recommendation of his relatives who held high office. This is meant to show what a tremendous power the English officer exercises in oppressing the poor under the protection of his relatives in high quarters. Then the people are taught to believe that such brutal officers cannot possibly exist under a representative government.

Such sweeping assertions by the writer of the pamphlet disclose his intention to set in motion seditious forces to destroy the peace of the country.

The hypothetical Maulvi asks the village headman to publish the stories of British oppression among peasants and others, through newspapers, with the view of forming native public opinion on the subject. Thus sensational stories showing grinding oppression exercised by the English on the subject-race are concocted to excite the masses against the Government. Is this acting in good faith? The loyal subjects of the Crown will not approve of such perfidious falsehoods. This treasonable policy has been persistently carried out by the Bengali Press. While every offender is held personally liable to punishment, this gang of sedition-mongers is allowed to write and talk rank sedition! The ominous reticence of a mild Government has spurred them on to overt and daring attempts at sedition. They have already come to regard the Government as a puppet in their hands.

(After commenting on the strictures on the Police contained in the pamphlet, the writer proceeds) :—

The pamphlet, if circulated in Central India, will bring a handsome reward to its writer from the notorious dacoit, Tantia Bhil. Police Superintendents are said to be the chief source of crime, the friends and accomplices of *budmashes*, and representative institutions are declared to be the panacea for these evils. Every false instance of oppression has been cited as a fair argument for getting rid of the present system of government. By denouncing the British Government as a grinding despotism, squandering away untold sums of money extorted from poor people and hastening their ruin, and by characterising public officers as heartless tyrants and warm friends of *budmashes*, the hypothetical Maulvi has apparently succeeded in inducing Rambakhsh to do his utmost to combine the people against the Government under the banner of the National Congress. I fear the next step would be to declare war against the Government. Common people do not know English law ; they are a host of semi-civilized and half-educated men, utterly ignorant of the first principles of Government and of the essential conditions of reform. They are *ignorant* in the broadest sense of the word, and, as a necessary consequence, haughty and excitable. Such people are sure to assist their leaders, or rather ringleaders, in their overt attempts at sedition.

I invite a refutation of my arguments. But
any one who undertakes to refute me, should not be
of the type of Mr. Hume, whose judgment has
been vitiated by old age.

Here I may ask whether, at the Congress meeting of December, 1887, Babu Surendranath Banerji
had not demanded the repeal of the Arms Act for
himself.   But it must be remembered that he is a
Bengali, so he wanted the ignorant and excitable
populace to be re-armed in order to assist him and
his party more effectively in achieving their end,
though I do not think the Government will give
them its forts and its bomb-shells.

Further on, Maulvi Fariduddin explains to
Rambakhsh the advantages of a representative
government like that of England, and strongly recommends the adoption of the representative system
for India.   In doing this, the writer deliberately
ignores the animosity caused by religious and other
differences among the different classes of the native
population.   In England fanaticism has completely
died out, but in India religious feelings are as
strong as ever and susceptible of excitement at a
breath.   Here the followers of one religion shudder
at the very thought of being overwhelmed by their
religious antagonists.   The writer of the pamphlet
seems to have had a short memory, or how could
he forget the Mohurrum and Daserah disturbances,
which only two years ago convulsed Delhi, Etawah,
and other cities, towns, and villages ?   How the
Jumma Masjid of Delhi was desecrated by the

Hindus, who tied a pig there to the inexpressible horror of the Faithful, who retaliated upon their enemies by slaughtering the sacred cow in a Hindu temple, must be fresh in the memory of every one. It was the strong arm of the British Government which prevented a general rising in many parts of the country and averted a dire calamity which threatened the social fabric with ruin at Delhi and elsewhere. Were it not for the opportune arrival at the Etawah Railway Station of the British troops proceeding to Burmah, nothing could have checked the riots at the former place, where the rioters, almost maddened by fierce religious emotions, were literally engaged in a bloody struggle when they were pushed back by the British soldiers at the point of the bayonet. Like the writer of the seditious pamphlet, Mr. Hume seems bent on earning a cheap notoriety by posing as a champion of oppressed humanity in India, just as his father, according to his own version of the story, paved the way for the supersession of a despotic by a constitutional government in Canada. But I cannot help observing that Mr. Hume desires to surpass even his father in revolutionising an empire perhaps ten times larger than the Dominion of Canada, if only the British Government would keep its eyes and ears shut against the storm that is brewing and if the Congresswallas succeed in stultifying English statesmen, and Sir William Hunter in electrifying the English people by his magic pen.

Then we find the deluded Rambakhsh trying his best to spread sedition among his friends and

neighbours, until not a single native of India is left
unmoved with a yearning for a radical change in the
principle of Government.

The hypothetical Maulvi is then made to say
that his own friends and neighbours are likewise
promulgating such views among traders, artisans,
and others, and that this is done in order to secure
unanimity, which is essential to the accomplishment
of the object in view. But what is the object in
view ? Surely the subversion of the present system
of Government. I wish they had induced the people to gather pebbles with which to pelt the British
out of the country ! No, I made a mistake. I should
have said that the Government of India would be
foolish enough to repeal the Arms Act in response
to the vehement protests of Messrs. Bepin Chandra
Pal and Surendranath Banerji, made with feminine
obstinacy. My European friends probably do not
know that *Trya Hat*, or feminine obstinacy, is a
prominent trait of native female character.

The part of the pamphlet of which I am now
speaking is the most treasonable, being an undis-
guised attempt to set every member of the subject-
race against the Government. I remember that a
Bengali paper accused Anti-Congressists of exciting
popular feelings, to which the *Pioneer* retorted by
saying that it was the partisans of the Congress who
were answerable for the spread of sedition among
the people, and every word of whose speeches and
writings betrayed a criminal intention to make every
native subject, from the prince to the peasant, a

sworn enemy of the British Government. Perhaps the writer in the Bengali Press never came across the pamphlet, every sentence of which breathes sedition, and which endeavours to combine all sections of the population in a regular league against the Government, with its countless ramifications spread all over the country ; for this is what the Maulvi says to Rambakhsh, that he would first establish a Central Political Association and then form minor or branch Associations in different parts of the country in order to teach the people such lessons. What purpose, it may be asked, can be served by exciting the illiterate masses, destitute alike of a sober judgment and elementary knowledge of law, except it be to create a mutiny ?

The writer insists on a large fund being raised by public subscription to enable one agent to be quartered at every village, elementary political tracts to be printed and distributed all over the country, hired men to travel all over the land preaching sedition, and sensational accounts of the political condition of India to be printed and sent to England.

It has been foolishly assumed that the British Government will remain deaf to this trumpet-call to mutiny. I know full well that by widely circulating all this seditious stuff, they are moving heaven and earth to enlist English sympathies on their side, and to pass utterly false and highly-coloured accounts of British oppression for true facts on the good people of England, who do not know the real state of things in this country. But I really do not believe that the

English nation would be foolish enough to listen to the mad ravings of a knot of professional agitators, and disregard the earnest protests of the peaceful and loyal people against the introduction of the representative system in a country where it cannot and will not work.

Even if it could be assumed that reckless philanthropists of the type of Messrs. Digby and Samuel Smith would succeed in fascinating the intellect of the English public, and that Mr. Slagg would also succeed in wringing out of a reluctant House of Commons a tardy concession to the Congressional demand for representative institutions " on pain of courting a grievous calamity," as Dr. Hunter forcibly puts it, will the brave races of India quietly submit to an arrangement which they consider highly prejudicial to their interests and under which they are sure to be overwhelmed by their rivals ?   I do not really bring myself to believe that the British Government will decide the fate of 250 millions of human beings committed to its care by Providence, according to the selfish views of isolated individuals like Messrs. W. C. Bonerji and Dada Bhai Nourojee ; for, to the sober judgment of all right-thinking men and sincere well-wishers of the people, a representative government is no less dangerous to a country like India than a fatal disease.

Further on, the writer boldly asserts that the whole native population sympathises with his party openly or secretly, and warns his co-adjutors against divulging the secrets of their party. How foolishly the Government is threatened with a revolution. I really cannot understand whether it is India or some other country that is painted in such gloomy colours. For aught I know, the writer of this silly pamphlet may have been a lunatic, or, if a sane man, he was a great liar. The National Congress has been almost pierced to death with sharp lances by gallant Musalmans and brave Rajputs in all parts of the country, and the stupid sedition-mongers, who foolishly imagine that the flimsy *saris* of the Bengalis will serve as iron walls to protect them from the dire consequences of their rash attempts at sedition, have been unanimously condemned as enemies alike of the Government and the country.

The writer of the pamphlet had better get his defective eye-sight restored to its normal condition by some ophthalmic surgeon, for he cannot evidently read newspapers.

Let the Government stand aside and leave the decision of the question of representative institutions to the discretion of the country, and you will see that the issue is finally settled, not by fictitious warfare on paper with pen and ink, but by actual war with the sword, the true arbiter of the fate of nations.

Further on, the writer predicts that a time will come when he and his party will win the battle and representative institutions will become an accomplished fact. This reminds one of a nursery tale about one *Shaikh Chilli*, the Alnascher of Oriental tales, who first bought hens which he sold and bought she-goats ; these too were sold in their turn, and a cow was bought ; this again was disposed of, and an elephant was purchased, the result being that all this buying and selling ended in a *fiasco !* I consider the crude notions of the *Congresswallas* mere childish freaks.   I would ask them whom they mean to fight ?   The British Government, to be sure. Well, if the Congresswallas came out victorious, then what would happen ?   Why, an Indian Chamber of Deputies would be formed with Mr. Hume for its President, Sir T. Madho Rao, Dewan Raghunath Rao, and Messrs. Surendranath Banerji and Budruddin Tyabji and other shining stars who move in the same orbit with them as Ministers. Then I would be sorely disappointed at not being pitchforked into the new-fledged Native Parliament. I am afraid I would be "hanged" as a traitor to my country at the bidding of the leaders of the republican party before distribution of public offices takes place in the new Republic.   But I think I should rejoice at the prospect of sharing the fate of the "unlucky host," as I would see brought to book with me, the whole of the Talukdars' party, my esteemed friends Munshi Imtiaz Ali and Munshi Athar Ali ; Munshi Ahmad Ali Shouk, Editor of the *Azad ;* Mr. W. B. Thompson, Editor of the *Express ;* Maulvi Abul Hasan, Munsarim, Office of the British Indian Association, so fiercely denounced by the Congress hero from Bombay at the meeting of the 7th July.   My friend Munshi Newal Kishore, *C.I.E.,* and his party, should also be ready to be led to the "gallows." It would be useless to mention names when millions of Muhammadans and Hindus, who love peace and abhor the spread of sedition through the mischievous propaganda, would share the fate of their more active compatriots in the coming mutiny.

I cannot help observing that the extremely lenient attitude taken by the Government towards this mischievous agitation has much aggravated the evil. This cold indifference on the part of the Government, if maintained too long, will, in the long run, turn the little fire, which may be put down to-day by some sprinkling of water, into a fearful conflagration which it will be difficult to extinguish by the application of a mighty fire-engine. That ignorant people are taught revolutionary doctrines and promising young men are trained to treason in a treasonable atmosphere, is an evil which should not be lightly disregarded.

Sir Auckland Colvin rightly observed in his Bareilly speech that raw youths, fresh from a college or school, are apt to form too high an opinion of themselves, imagining that they are perfectly fit to do all sorts of work, and that those able and ex-perienced men who lived in bygone times or who are still living, were all fools.

I am at a loss to know in what will all this in-citement to sedition end. I cannot help laughing at those of my countrymen who are insane enough to pelt the living Lion in the foolish hope that they will kill him by the mere pelting!

Now, I must bring my review of the seditious pamphlet to a close. I know full well that my opponents will abuse me to their hearts' content, but my conscience has compelled me to speak out the truth in defiance of all calumny and abuse. I most undoubtedly regard these overt attempts at sedition as likely to destroy the peace of the country, like a thunderbolt burning down a smiling garden. On a future occasion I shall publish my views on the Congress movement.

MUHAMMAD NUSRAT ALI,

Assistant Secy., B. I. Association, Oudh.

APPENDIX.

THE
UNITED INDIAN PATRIOTIC ASSOCIATION.

RULES.

I. THIS Association shall be called "THE UNITED INDIAN PATRIOTIC ASSOCIATION."

II. Its objects shall be :—

(*a*). To publish and circulate pamphlets and other papers for information of members of Parliament, English journals, and the people of Great Britain, in which those misstatements will be pointed out by which the supporters of the Indian National Congress have wrongfully attempted to convince the English people that all the nations of India and the Indian Chiefs and Rulers agree with the aims and objects of the National Congress.

(*b*). To inform members of Parliament and the newspapers of Great Britain and its people by the same means of the opinions of Muhammadans in general, of the Islamia Anjumans, and of those Hindus and their Societies which are opposed to the objects of the National Congress.

(*c*). To strive to preserve peace in India, and to strengthen the British Rule, and to remove those bad feelings from the hearts of the

Indian people which the supporters of the Congress are stirring up throughout the country, and by which great dissatisfaction is being raised among the people against the British Government.

III. Indian Chiefs and Rulers who sympathise with the objects of the Association will be requested to become Patrons of the Association.

IV. Subject to Rule V, any person, of whatever race or creed, agreeing with the objects of the Association, may become a member of the Association on payment, in advance, of an annual subscription of from Rs. 12 to Rs. 60, according to the wish of the subscriber.

V. No person who is a paid Government servant can become a member of the Association.

VI. Donations will be accepted from members and others anxious to help the work of the Association. The names of donors who are not members will be published in a separate list.

VII. The names of Islamia Anjumans and Hindu Societies which may have expressed their sympathy with the objects of the Association will be published in a separate list.

VIII. The list containing the names of members, donors and Anjumans sympathising with the Association will be sent with every pamphlet to England for circulation.

IX. Members who have subscribed at the rate of Rs. 60 per annum will be supplied, free of cost, with copies of all pamphlets which may be printed by the Association for circulation in England. Other persons may purchase such pamphlets.

X. An Annual Report of the work of the Association, including an account of income and expenditure, will be sent, free of cost, to all members and the above-mentioned Societies.

XI. A European gentleman will be appointed as an Editor to assist in the preparation and publication of pamphlets.

XII. The contents of the pamphlets published shall be as follows :—

(*a*). Articles and news selected from Indian papers sympathising with the Association and translations from Vernacular papers.

(*b*). The resolutions and opinions of meetings of Muhammadans and Hindus which may have expressed sympathy with the objects of the Association.

(*c*). Articles, lectures, and essays by members and non-members in support of the objects of the Association. The names of the writers will be published, except in cases when the writer does not wish his name to be published and the gentlemen in charge of the preparation of pamphlets agree to its anonymous publication.

XIII. Some members of the Association will be selected, who, in conjunction with the Editor, will select and sanction the publication of pamphlets, &c.

XIV. All communications should be addressed to the Hon'ble Sir Syed Ahmed, Khan Bahadur, *K. C. S. I.*, at Aligarh, who will act as Honorary Secretary and Treasurer till further arrangements have been made.

(Sd.) SYED AHMED,
Honorary Secretary.

PATRONS.

HIS HIGHNESS THE NIZAM OF HYDERABAD (DECCAN).

Letter of His Highness's Prime Minister, Sir Asman Jah, to the Secretary of the Association, Hyderabad (Deccan), dated 29th September, 1888.

MY DEAR SIR SYED AHMED,—On behalf of His Highness and by his command I have much pleasure in enclosing a cheque for Rs. 4,000 towards the United Indian Patriotic Association which you and other well-wishers of the country have founded. I am to add that the aims and objects of the Association have His Highness's fullest sympathy.

I remain,

My dear Sir Syed Ahmed,

Yours sincerely,

(Sd.) ASMAN JAH.

HIS EXCELLENCY NAWAB SIR SALAR JUNG, *K. C. I. E.*

His Excellency Nawab Sir Salar Jung, K. C. I. E.'s letter to the Secretary of the Association is as follows :—

POONA ;

2nd September, 1888.

MY DEAR SIR SYED AHMED,—I have to acknowledge with thanks your letter setting forth the nature and aims of the United Indian Patriotic Association. I feel highly gratified at being elected a patron of the Association, and I take this opportunity of expressing my cordial approval of the energetic and timely steps which you have taken to counteract the mischievous teachings of the body which has arrogated to itself the title of the Indian National Congress. That the Congress in question is a truly national or representative association, no one acquainted with the elements composing it, or the objects which it has set before itself, can for a moment believe. Indeed, a representative body is in the present day, at any rate, utterly inconceivable, when one considers the heterogeneous population of India, with its diversities of creed, custom, character, and traditional sympathies and antipathies. Whether it will become a possibility in the future we need not here stop to inquire. What we have to deal with is the present, and in the present what do we find ? A Government, which—whatever may be its shortcomings—is beyond doubt not only far superior to any that the land has ever had under former rulers, but which is decidedly superior to most of those now existing in what are universally admitted to be the advanced countries of the West. For, in which of the countries of Europe does the subject enjoy greater liberty of speech and action ; in how many is he more lightly taxed, and where are his rights better protected by law, or greater toleration manifested towards his religion and social usages than in India ? The agitators forget that the Government of India, as at present constituted, is no crude and novel experiment in administration, but is the outcome of historical circumstances and years of earnest, philanthropic and thoughtful elaboration, while the long interval of peace, which the country has enjoyed under a just and impartial rule, has afforded opportunities for the development of a condition of prosperity which, we may be sure, is fully appreciated by the immense majority of the people.

We have it on high authority that the evils which men do live after them, and it is a matter of sincere regret that this unfortunate agitation should have gone the length it has

done, for even should the movement, which, as you know, is
not quite spontaneous, die out, the pamphlets, catechisms,
and tracts now being sown broadcast by the emissaries of
the Congress are not likely to be wholly without effect, and
the least of the evils to be appreciated from this misguided
and misleading propagandism is the fostering of a spirit of
discontent and restlessness amongst the masses which may
hereafter give serious trouble to the Government.

It is gratifying, however, to find that numbers of
Muhammadans of high culture and social position have refused to countenance the Congress from the first, while
others, who had joined it without full consideration, with-
drew after a closer scrutiny had revealed to them the true
character and tendency of the movement to which they
had given their adhesion. The power of the Government
of India, and, in particular, its ability to act with prompti-
tude and energy in times of emergency, depend entirely
upon the centralisation of authority. Those Muhammadans
who have studied the history of the Musalman dynasties
that formerly held sway in India, are fully cognisant of
this fact, and to them, as well as to numbers of their
enlightened Hindu brethren, the demands and pretensions
of the Congress must appear dangerous and impracticable.
For the nature of the Indians, and for that matter of most
Oriental people, is averse to sudden and violent changes
of any kind. What they have been accustomed to, what
they have contentedly lived under for years, to that they
will adhere persistently. They have a settled, and to some
extent a natural and wholesome, repugnance to the unsuit-
able, the unknown, and the untried. If political experi-
ments are looked upon with suspicion in Europe, they are
infinitely more unpopular here. Exotic notions regarding
the parliamentary form of government are not likely to
take root in India until our circumstances and conditions
approach more nearly to those existing in England, and

this is not to be expected for many years to come. The great majority of the people of this country know nothing of the theories of representative institutions which appear to be the stock-in-trade of the Congress. Wishing you every success in the useful and patriotic movement which you have initiated, and in promoting which I feel confident that you will have the assistance and the best sympathies of all who understand the real interest and necessities of India, whatever be their creed or nationality.

I remain, with kind regards,

Yours sincerely,

(Sd.) SALAR JUNG.

HIS HIGHNESS THE MAHARAJA OF CHHATARPUR.

LIST OF MEMBERS.

FIFTY-THREE Muhammadan Associations, a list of which is given hereafter, have been affiliated to the Patriotic Association. All their members are therefore members of this Association indirectly. The list would, however, be far too lengthy if we gave the names of these members, and we therefore quote the names of those only who have directly become members of this Association and have given subscriptions or donations towards its funds.

	DONORS AND MEMBERS.	Rs.
(1).—	His Highness the Nizam of Hyderabad	4,000
(2).—	Nawab Imad-ud-Dowlah, Maulvi Syed Hosain Bilgrami, Ali Yar Khan Bahadur, Motaman Jung	500
(3).—	His Highness the Maharaja of Chhatarpur	400
(4).—	Thakur Chunder Pal Singh, Talukdar of Kari Harsatana (Oudh)	160
(5).—	Hon'ble Maharaja Pertab Narain Singh, Bahadur, Talukdar of Mahdona, Zila Fyzabad (Oudh),	200
(6).—	Koer Misr Har Charan, Raïs, Bareilly (N.-W. P.),	160

MEMBERS.

(7).—Nawab Intisar Jung, Maulvi Mahomed Mushtak Husain, Bahadur, Officiating Political and Finance Secretary to the Government of His Highness the Nizam, Hyderabad (Deccan).

(8).—Syed Mir Zahur Husain Sahib, Vakil, High Court, Allahabad, Raïs, Moradabad (N.-W. P.).

(9).—Munshi Mahomed Imtiaz Ali Sahib, Raïs, Kakauri (Oudh), Vakil and Legal Adviser to the Anjuman-i-Talukdaran (Oudh).

(10).—Khan Bahadur Chaudhri Mahomed Nusrat Ali Sahib, Talukdar, Sandhila (Oudh), and Assistant Secretary, Anjuman-i-Talukdaran (Oudh).

(11).—Theodore Beck, Esq., Principal, Mahomedan Anglo-
Oriental College, Aligarh (N.-W.P.).

(12).—The Hon'ble Sir Syed Ahmed, Khan Bahadur,
K.C.S.I., of Aligarh (N.-W. P.).

(13).—Wazir-ud-Dowlah, Mudabbirul Mulk, Khalifa Syed
Mahomed Hasan Khan, Bahadur, Prime Minister
of Patiala State (Punjab).

(14).—Mashir-ud-Dowlah, Mumtazul Mulk, Khalifa Syed
Mahomed Husain Khan, Bahadur, Foreign Minister of Patiala State (Punjab).

(15).—Khan Bahadur Kazi Syed Raza Husain Sahib,
Raïs, Patna (Bengal).

(16).—Raja Rampal Singh Sahib, Talukdar of Rampore,
Siroli (Oudh).

(17).—Sheikh Ghulam Mustafa Sahib, Raïs of Mao, Zila
Allahabad (N.-W. P.).

(18).—Mr. F. Beauclerk, late Captain, Royal Engineers,
Naval and Military Club, 94 Piccadilly, and U. S.
Club, Calcutta, Hyderabad (Deccan).

(19).—Shams-ul-Ulama, Khan Bahadur, Maulvi Mahomed
Zaka-ul-lah Sahib, Raïs of Delhi (Punjab).

(20).—Koer Mahomed Lutf Ali Khan, Bahadur, Raïs,
Talibnagar, Member, Council of Rampore State
(N.-W. P.).

(21).—Nawab Abdul Majid Khan, Bahadur, *C.I.E.*, of
Lahore (Punjab).

(22).—Sheikh Rahim Baksh Sahib, Malikul Tujjar and
Honorary Magistrate, Lahore (Punjab).

(23).—Mian Karim Baksh Sahib, Municipal Commissioner,
Lahore (Punjab).

(24).—Sheikh Mahomed Hasan Sahib, son of Sheikh
Sandhey Khan Sahib, Raïs, Hoshiarpore and
Lahore (Punjab).

(25).—Chaudhri Sher Mahomed Sahib, Raïs, Mian-Mir,
Lahore (Punjab).

(26).—Maulvi Hafiz Mahomed Ismail Sahib, Raïs, and Great Maulvi and Imam Jama Masjid, Aligarh (N.-W. P.).

(27).—Khan Bahadur Maulvi Mahomed Ibrahim Sahib, Vice-President, Municipal Board, Jaunpore (N.-W. P.).

(28).—Khan Bahadur Mahomed Barkat Ali Khan Sahib, General Secretary, Anjuman-i-Islam, Lahore (Punjab).

(29).—Mumtaz-ud-Dowlah Nawab Sir Mahomed Faiz Ali Khan, Bahadur, *K.C.S.I.*, Raïs, Pahasu, Zila Bulandshahr (N.-W. P.).

(30).—Haji Mahomed Mustafa Khan Sahib, Raïs, Buragaon, Zila Aligarh (N.-W. P.).

(31).—Khan Bahadur Mahomed Kadir Baksh Khan Sahib, Honorary Extra-Assistant Commissioner, Qasur (Punjab).

(32).—Hon'ble Rana Sir Shankar Baksh Singh Sahib, Bahadur, *K.C.S.I.*, Talukdar, Khajurgaon, Rae-Bareli (Oudh).

(33).—Raja Jagmohan Singh Sahib, Talukdar, Chanda-pore, Zila Rae-Bareli (Oudh).

(34).—Chaudhri Mahomed Azim Sahib, Talukdar, Kakrali, Zila Hardoi (Oudh).

(35).—Raja Tasadduq Rasul Khan Sahib, Talukdar, Jahan-girabad, Zila Bara-Banki (Oudh).

(36).—Sheikh Enayet-ul-lah Sahib, Talukdar, Sidanpore, Zila Bara-Banki (Oudh).

(37).—Munshi Mahomed Athar Ali Sahib, Vakil, and Raïs of Kakauri (Oudh).

(38).—Raja Sayed Shaban Ali Khan Sahib, Talukdar of Salimpore, Zila Lucknow (Oudh).

(39).—Bhia Tirbhawandip Narain Pandey, Talukdar of Singha Chanda, Zila Gonda (Oudh).

(40).—Syed Shah Abul Hasan Sahib (Motamid), Agent, Balrampore State.

(41).—Sheikh Ahmed Husain Khan Sahib, Raïs of Piryawan, Zila Partabgarh (Oudh).

(42).—Shahzada Mirza Sulaiman Qadr Bahadur, brother of Wajid Ali Shah, late King of Oudh.

(43).—Muhtashim-ud-Dowlah, Muazzam-ul-Mulk Shahzada Mirza Mahomed Mahdi Ali Khan, Bahadur, Nadir Jung of the Royal Family of Oudh.

(44).—Maulvi Syed Abul Hasan Sahib, Translator of Anjuman-i-Hind (Oudh).

(45).—Raja Durga Parshad Sahib of Sandhila (Oudh).

(46).—Munshi Ahmed Ali Sahib (Shauk), Proprietor of the " *Azad*," Lucknow (Oudh).

(47).—Qazi Khalil-ud-din Ahmed Sahib, son of the late Qazi Said-ud-din Ahmed, Khan Bahadur, Raïs of Biswan, Zila Sitapur (Oudh).

(48).—Qazi Bakhsish Ilahi Sahib, Raïs of Biswan, Zila Sitapore (Oudh).

(49).—Nawab Ahmad-ul-lah, Khan Bahadur, of Meerut.

(50).—Maulvi Khwaja Mahomed Yusaf Sahib of Aligarh (N.-W. P.).

(51).—Khwaja Wahidjan Sahib, Landholder, Gya.

(52).—Maulvi Sheikh Habib-ul-lah Sahib, Pleader, Azamgarh (N.-W. P.).

(53).—Koer Mahomed Faiyaz Ali Khan Sahib of Pahasu, Zila Bulandshahr (N.-W. P.).

(54).—Syed Mahomed Mir Sahib of Delhi, Pleader, Judge's Court, Meerut.

(55).—Maulvi Yusaf Ali Sahib of Bhaptiahi, district Bhagalpore.

(56).—Prince Mirza Sulaiman Shah Bahadur, Gorkani, of Delhi, of the old Royal Family.

(57).—Maulvi Syed Mahomed Nuh Sahib, Raïs of Machhlishahr, Zila Jaunpore (N.-W. P.).

(58).—Maulvi Syed Ali Husain Sahib, Raïs of Jaunpore (N.-W. P.).

(59).—Mufti Hyder Husain Sahib, Member, District Board, and Raïs of Jaunpore (N.-W. P.).

(60).—Maulvi Syed Mahomed Sahib, Pleader, Civil Court, Jaunpore, and Raïs of Kheta-Sarai.

(61).—Munshi Abdul Karim Sahib, Secretary, Anjuman-i-Ahbab, Bombay.

(62).—Prince Asman Jah, Bahadur, son of the late King of Oudh, Calcutta.

(63).—Mahomed Hyder Ali Khan Sahib, Raïs of Shah-jahanpore (N.-W. P.).

(64).—Mahomed Mansur Shah Khan Sahib, Pleader, Ali-garh (N.-W. P.).

(65).—Munshi Mahomed Rahmat-ul-lah Sahib (Rād), Proprietor of the "*Alam-i-Taswir,*" Cawnpore (N.-W. P.).

(66).—Raja Hari Har Datt Dubey, Bahadur, of Jaunpore (N.-W. P.).

(67).—Maulvi Mahomed Ali Sahib, Raïs, Machhlishahr, Zila Jaunpore (N.-W. P.).

(68).—Maulvi Mahomed Said Khan Sahib, Pleader, Jaun-pore (N.-W. P.).

(69).—Maulvi Farid-ul-Haq Sahib, Pleader, Jaunpore (N.-W. P.).

(70).—Mahomed Muhsin Ali Khan Sahib, son of the Talukdar of Jagore (Oudh).

(71).—Lala Eshar Dass Sahib, Collector, Kapurthala State (Punjab).

(72).—Lala Bhagwan Das Sahib, Mir Munshi, Kapurthala State (Punjab).

(73).—Maulvi Abu Said Mahomed Husain Sahib, Editor of the "*Eshaatul Sunna,*" Lahore (Punjab).

(74).—Hon'ble Maharaja Partab Narain Singh, Bahadur, Talukdar of Mahdona, Zila Fyzabad (Oudh).

(75).—Sheikh Abdul Ghaffar Sahib, Raïs and Pleader, Civil Court, Rae-Bareli (Oudh).

(76).—Munshi Shahab-ud-din Sahib, Raïs and Pleader, Civil Court, Rae-Bareli (Oudh).

(77).—Thakur Har Har Baksh Singh Sahib, Talukdar of Sarorah, Zila Sitapore (Oudh).

(78).—Abdul Majid, Esq., Barrister-at-Law and Raïs of Jaunpore (N.-W. P.).

(79).—Raja Uday Partab Singh, Bahadur, Raja of Bhinga (Oudh).

(80).—Maulvi Abdul Ghani Sahib, Raïs of Saharanpore (N.-W. P.).

(81).—Syed Jaffar Husain Sahib, Appellate Judge, Kota (Rajputana).

(82.)—Mahomed Salam-ul-lah Khan of Devalghat of Baldova (Berar), Honorary Magistrate.

(83).—Maulvi Ikbal Ali Sahib, Judge of High Court of H. H. the Nizam, Hyderabad (Deccan).

(84).—Nawab Mahomed Naim Khan Sahib, Raïs of Kailaspur, Zila Saharanpore (N.-W. P.).

(85).—Mahomed Muzzammil-ul-lah Khan Sahib, Raïs of Bhikampore, Zila Aligarh (N.-W. P.).

(86).—Haji Mahomed Yusaf Khan Sahib, Raïs of Dataoli, Zila Aligarh (N.-W. P.).

(87).—Shams-ul-Ulama Maulvi Mahomed Hasan Sahib, Raïs of Patna.

(88).—Mahomed Hadi Yar Khan Sahib, Raïs of Dadon, Zila Aligarh (N.-W. P.).

(89).—Haji Mahomed Ismail Khan Sahib, Raïs of Dataoli, Zila Aligarh (N.-W. P.).

(90).—Nawab Mahomed Ali Khan Sahib, Raïs of Jahangirabad, Zila Bulandshahr (N.-W. P.).

(91).—Raja Syed Baqar Ali Khan Sahib, C. I. E., Raïs of Pindrawal, Zila Bulandshahr (N.-W. P.).

(92).—Raja Jung Bahadur Khan Sahib, Bahadur, C. I. E., Raïs of Nanpara, Zila Bahraich (Oudh).

(93).—Mahomed Yakub Khan Sahib, Raïs of Dataoli, Zila Aligarh (N.-W. P.).

(94).—Haji Ahmed Said Khan Sahib, Raïs of Bhikampore, Zila Aligarh (N.-W. P.).

(95).—Munshi Mahomed Irtiza Ali Sahib, Raïs of Kakauri (Oudh).

(96).—Maulvi Mahomed Lutf-ul-lah Sahib, Raïs of Pilkhana, Zila Aligarh (N.-W. P.).

(97).—Mir Ashiq Ali Sahib, Raïs of Jalali, Zila Aligarh (N.-W. P.).

(98).—Nawab Khwaja Sharf-ud-din Ahmed Khan, Raïs of Delhi.

(99).—Joseph Beck, Esq., London.

(100).—A. G. Pears, Esq., C.E., Sagra viâ Sambalpur, C.P.

(101).—C. B. Ewatt, Esq., C.E., Sagra viâ Sambalpur, C.P.

(102).—Raja Kishan Kumar of Bilari.

(103).—Maulvi Fida Ali Sahib, Pleader, Meerut.

(104).—Sheikh Walayat Ali Sahib, Pleader, Meerut.

(105).—Syed Najm-ud-din Khan Sahib, Raïs of Sirdhana, Zila Meerut.

(106).—Chaudhri Rustam Khan Sahib, Raïs of Khurja, Zila Bulandshahr.

(107).—Hafiz Hamid Husain Khan Sahib, Raïs of Meerut.

(108).—Mahomed Umarjan Khan Sahib, Raïs of Meerut.

(109).—Syed Kasim Ali Sahib, Raïs of Meerut.

DONORS (NON-MEMBERS).	Rs.	a.
Raja Shimbhu Narain Singh, Bahadur, of Benares ...	10	0
Doctor Sadrul Haq, of Patna	2	8

LIST OF AFFILIATED MUHAMMADAN ASSOCIATIONS.

THE Secretary of the United Indian Patriotic Association sent a circular to various Muhammadan Anjumans, stating therein the objects of the United Indian Patriotic Association, and making the request that the circular be laid before the Anjumans ; and that if they agreed with these objects they should allow their names to be entered in the list of Anjumans sympathising with the Association. The following Anjumans have expressed their concurrence with the aims of the Association :—

1. *Anjuman Islamia, Lahore, Punjab.*—The President of this Anjuman is Nawab Abdul Majid, Khan Bahadur, *C.I.E.*; General Secretary, Khan Bahadur Mahomed Barkat Ali Khan ; and Financial Secretary, Mahomed Fazl-ud-din.

A general meeting of this Association was held on August 26th, and all the members concurred in the opinion that Muhammadans should hold aloof from the Indian National Congress and not join in its inexpedient pro-posals. The following two resolutions were passed :—

(1). That the Anjuman Islamia, as a united body, become a member of the United Indian Patriotic Association.

(2). That inasmuch as the aims of the National Congress are diametrically opposite to those of the Anjuman Islamia, anyone favouring the cause of the Congress will be considered as no longer fit to continue a member of the aforesaid Anjuman.

2. *Anjuman Islamia Haqani, Ludhiana, Punjab.*— Maulvi Nur Mahomed, the Secretary of the Anjuman, sent a letter, on September 1st, to the Secretary of the United Indian Patriotic Association, stating that all members of

the Anjuman agreed with the objects of the United Indian Patriotic Association.

3. *The Central National Muhammadan Association of Calcutta.*—A meeting of the Committee of Management of the Central Muhammadan Association of Calcutta was held on September 2nd, and it was resolved " that the Hon'ble Sir Syed Ahmed, Khan Bahadur, *K.C.S.I.*, be informed that the Central National Muhammadan Association has every sympathy with the objects of the United Indian Patriotic Association."

4. *Anjuman Islamia, Amritsar, Punjab.*—A meeting of the Anjuman was called on September 2nd, and the following resolutions were passed :—

(1). Proposed by Khan Bahadur Shaikh Gholam Hasan and seconded by Khwaja Zahur Shah, that the Anjuman entirely agrees with the aims and objects of the United Indian Patriotic Association.

(2). Proposed by Khan Bahadur Haji Khan Mahomed Shah and seconded by Hafiz Gholam Jilani, that if any member of the Anjuman become a member of the National Congress, or attend any meeting convened by any supporter of the National Congress, he should be expelled from the Anjuman.

(3). Proposed by Shaikh Ala Bakhsh and seconded by Khwaja Mehar Shah, that it is the duty of the Anjuman to enlighten the public as to the evils likely to befall the country, the peace of the country, and Muhammadans from the National Congress ; and further, to explain the benefits likely to arise from the United Indian Patriotic Association.

(4). Proposed by Khan Bahadur Shaikh Gholam Hasan and seconded by Khwaja Yusaf Shah, that a copy of these resolutions be forwarded to the Secretary of the United Indian Patriotic Association.

5. *Anjuman Himayat Islam, Amritsar, Punjab.*—A meeting of the Anjuman was held on September 2nd, and the following resolution was passed :—

" That inasmuch as the Indian National Congress is opposed to the policy of the Government and is destructive of friendship between the different peoples of India, and is prejudicial to the peace of the country, this Anjuman expresses its entire agreement with the United Indian Patriotic Association and its complete hostility to the Indian National Congress, and looks on the proposals of the latter as poison for the Muhammadan community."

6. *Anjuman Islamia Bareilly, North-Western Provinces.*—The Secretary of the Anjuman sent a letter, dated September 7th, to the Secretary of the United Indian Patriotic Association, stating that the Anjuman had decided that it was expedient neither for it nor for any other Anjuman to join the National Congress. Nawab Mahomed Abdul Aziz Khan, a member of the Anjuman, made a speech, in which he spoke in the strongest terms against Muhammadans joining the Congress, saying that it was extremely injurious and dangerous for the peace of the country.

7. *The National Muhammadan Association, Bhagalpur, Bengal.*—A letter, dated September 6th, was sent by the Secretary of this Association to the Secretary of the United Indian Patriotic Association, stating the desire of the National Muhammadan Association of Bhagalpur to join the United Indian Patriotic Association.

8. *Anjuman Islamia, Chapra, zila Sarun, Bengal.*— Maulvi Syed Mahomed Shafi, Secretary of this Anjuman, sent a letter to the Secretary of the United Indian Patriotic Association, stating that the Anjuman entirely agreed with the objects of the United Indian Patriotic Association.

9. *Anjuman Ilmi, Budaon, North-Western Provinces.*— President of the Anjuman, Maulvi Tofail Ahmed ; Vice-

President, Kazi Ali Ahmed (Mahmud-ul-lah Shah); Secretary, Hafiz Fazi-i-lkram. It was decided that the Anjuman entirely agreed with the aims of the United Indian Patriotic Association.

10. *Anjuman Islamia, Budaon, North-Western Provinces.*—President of the Anjuman, Munshi Tajammul Hosain ; Secretary, Maulvi Hafiz Zahir Ahmed Shah. The Anjuman decided to join the United Indian Patriotic Association.

11. *The Jubilee Muhammadan Association, Budaon, North-Western Provinces.*—President, Kazi Ali Ahmed (Mahmud-ul-lah Shah); Secretary, Munshi Afzal Ali. The Anjuman decided to join the United Indian Patriotic Association.

12. *Anjuman Islamia, Bankipur, Bengal.*—A general meeting of Muhammadans was held by the Anjuman Islamia of Bankipur on September 9th. About two thousand Muhammadans were present, representing the aristocracy, the gentry, the alims, pleaders and mukhtars, merchants and shop-keepers, and the students of the local college and schools. All the influential Muhammadans of Patna, except one, were present or sent letters expressing their sympathy with the object of the meeting. The following resolutions were unanimously passed :—

(1). Moved by Khan Bahadur Maulvi Khoda Bakhsh Khan, pleader, and seconded by Khan Bahadur Maulvi Syed Fazl Imam, and supported by Maulvi Syed Rahim-ud-din, Editor, " *Alpunch* "—" That the Anjuman considers that the aims and objects of the so-called National Congress would, if carried out, vitally injure Muhammadan interests and the Muhammadan religion."

(2). Moved by Khan Bahadur Maulvi Syed Fazl Imam and seconded by Maulvi Syed Mahomed Hasan, *B. A.*, Editor, "*Patna Institute Gazette*," and supported by Maulvi Abdul Ghani, pleader—" That this Anjuman is wholly opposed to the Congress, and has not the least sympathy with it."

(3). Moved by Khan Bahadur Syed Kazi Raza Hosain and seconded by Maulvi Mahomed Kaim, Secretary, Jalsa Hami Islam, and supported by Maulvi Mahomed Yusaf Hosain, Secretary, Anjuman Irtibat ; Maulvi Syed Mahomed Hasan, *B. A.*, Editor, "*Patna Institute Gazette*" ; Maulvi Syed Rahim-ud-din, Editor, "*Alpunch*" ; and Maulvi Abid Hosain, Editor, " *Anis* "—" That this Anjuman fully sympathises with the United Indian Patriotic Association."

13. *Majlis Islamia, Ludhiana, Punjab.*—On September 2nd a meeting of this Anjuman was held at the house of Sirdar Ali Mahomed Khan, at which it was resolved that the Anjuman join the United Indian Patriotic Association.

14. *Anjuman Islamia, Dindigul, Madras.*—On September 5th a meeting was held, at which it was resolved that as this Anjuman neither in the past joined the National Congress nor sent a delegate, so in the present it has no sympathy with it, but agrees with the objects of the United Indian Patriotic Association.

15. *Branch National Muhammadan Association, Midnapur, Bengal.*—At a meeting held on September 9th, it was resolved—" That this Branch National Muhammadan Association fully sympathises with the aims and objects of the United Indian Patriotic Association."

16. *Majlis Islamia, Meerut, North-Western Provinces.*—President, Nawab Ahmed-ul-lah Khan ; Vice-President, Maulvi Fida Ali ; Secretary, Syed Mahomed Mir. On September 9th a meeting of this Anjuman was held, and the following resolutions were passed :—

(1). That the Association be affiliated to the United Indian Patriotic Association for the purpose of strengthening the opposition to the National Congress.

(2). That the Association and the Muhammadans of the district generally consider the objects of the said Congress to be unwise and unsuited to the country.

17. *Anjuman Islamia, Mymensing, Eastern Bengal.*— A meeting of this Anjuman was recently held, at which it was unanimously resolved—" That this Anjuman does not think it advisable to join or to co-operate with the Babus in their Congress movement."

18. *Branch Muhammadan Association, Shaikhpura, Behar.*—On August 28th a meeting of this Association was held, at which it was decided that the Association was opposed to the National Congress, and agreed with the aims of the United Indian Patriotic Association.

19. *Anjuman Islamia, Gujrat, Punjab.*—On September 9th a general meeting was held, at which it was resolved that the Anjuman was entirely opposed to every proposal of the National Congress, and was desirous of joining it in no kind of way.

20. *Anjuman Islamia, Jhajhar, District Rohtak, Punjab.*—On September 9th a meeting of this Association was held, at which it was decided that the objects of the National Congress were prejudicial to the interests of Muhammadans and to the peace of the country ; and that the Anjuman was therefore opposed to the proposals of the National Congress, and agreed with the United Indian Patriotic Association.

21. *Muhammadan Anjuman Mufid-i-Am, Qasur, Punjab.*—President, Munshi Kadir Baksh Khan. On September 7th a meeting of this Anjuman was held, at which the following resolutions were passed :—

(1). That this Anjuman unanimously sympathises with the United Indian Patriotic Association.

(2). That if a member of this Anjuman joins the National Congress he be excluded from the Anjuman.

22. *Anjuman Islamia, Jubbulpore, Central Provinces.*— On September 8th a meeting of this Anjuman was held, at which the following resolutions were passed :—

(1). That the differences amongst the people of India as regards their religion, manners and customs, the variety of wants and interests which their respective circumstances create, and their ignorance of politics, disqualify them from forming a body such as the National Congress. The good of the Muhammadans lies in helping the Government to do what it has been doing in the past—educating us and giving us more and more power as our knowledge advanced.

(2). In the present state of the Muhammadan society, especially in a country like India, where the number of Hindus and their influence predominate, the vote system, which is the fundamental principle of the Congress, is highly injurious to the Muhammadans : and if the Government pleases to introduce such a system in the administration, the oppression of the minority by the majority will be established, which is worse than the most aristocratic Government ; for, in the former case, the oppressed will look in vain for sympathy to the public. The concrete example of such a measure will be found in the local and municipal self-government, where the Muhammadans are disproportionally represented.

(3). The chief promoters of the Congress are Bengalis, and the Muhammadan community of India has kept aloof from it, and those who have joined are not influential amongst us, nor worthy of being called our leaders. The Muhammadans of this place should therefore stand apart from this agitation.

23. *Anjuman Islamia, Wazirabad, Punjab.*—President, Raja Faqir-ul-lah, Khan Bahadur ; Secretary, Hakim Ali Ahmed. A meeting of this Anjuman was

held on September 12th, and the following resolutions
were passed :—

(1). That this meeting is entirely opposed to the
objects of the National Congress.

(2). That this meeting entirely agrees and sympathises with the aims of the Indian United Patriotic
Association.

24. *Anjuman Himayat-i-Islam, Lahore, Punjab.*—
The Secretary wrote to the Secretary of the United Indian
Patriotic Association to say that the Anjuman was entirely opposed to the National Congress, and had refused to
send delegates to that body in 1887.

25. *Anjuman Hamdardi, Amritsar, Punjab.*—On September 18th a meeting of this Anjuman was held, at which
it was decided that the Anjuman was entirely opposed
to the National Congress and agreed with the United
Indian Patriotic Association.

26. *Anjuman Muinul Islam, Ajmere, Rajputana.*—
On September 18th a meeting of this Anjuman was held,
at which it was agreed that all members of the Anjuman
were against the National Congress, and sympathised with
the United Indian Patriotic Association.

27. *Majlis-i-Islam, Bangalore, and Majlis-i-Islam,
Ahsan, Mysore.*—On September 9th a united meeting of
these two Anjumans was held, at which the following
resolutions were passed :—

(1). That this meeting entirely agrees with Sir Syed
Ahmed's views, and is opposed to the National Congress.

(2). That the Majlis-i-Islam, Bangalore, and its
branch, the Majlis-i-Islam, Ahsan, sympathise with the
United Indian Patriotic Association.

The Secretary further wrote to the effect that Hindus
at their late Congress in Madras selected the name of
Mahomed Kasim, an honourable member of the Majlis, as
one of their delegates, but that he declined the honour.

28. *Anjuman Islamia, Cawnpore, North-Western Provinces.*—A meeting of this Anjuman was held on Friday, September 7th, in the mosque of Imaman Sirdar, at which 500 Muhammadans were present. It was unanimously decided that all present were not only opposed to the National Congress, but hated it from their hearts, because the National Congress would in the future be a cause of great misfortune and suffering for Muhammadans.

29. *Anjuman-i-Babussalam, Piryaman, Partabgarh, Oudh.*—A meeting of this Anjuman was held on September 18th, at which the following resolution was passed :—

"That this Anjuman is utterly opposed to the National Congress and entirely agrees with all the aims of the United Indian Patriotic Association, and that all members thank the United Indian Patriotic Association, and pray God that He may send His blessings on the work of the Association."

30. *National Muhammadan Association, Branch Ellore, Madras.*—On September 12th a meeting of this Association was held in the house of the Kazi of the city, at which it was decided that all members were opposed to the National Congress, and agreed with the opinions of Sir Syed Ahmed and the aims of the United Indian Patriotic Association.

31. *Anjuman Darussalam, Lucknow, Oudh.*—The Secretary of this Anjuman wrote to say that the Anjuman agreed with the United Indian Patriotic Association and was opposed to the National Congress, believing it to be very harmful, not only for Muhammadans but for the whole people of India ; and that the Anjuman had worked hard against the Congress in Lucknow, the great meeting of 20,000 people on May 6th having been held under its auspices.

32. *Anjuman Islamia, Mooltan, Punjab.*—A meeting of this Anjuman was held on September 23rd, at which the following resolutions were passed :—

(1). That the principle of the Anjuman is to abstain from interference in politics, and therefore it cannot agree with the agitation of the National Congress.

(2). Inasmuch as the object of the United Indian Patriotic Association is to show that the Muhammadans do not join the National Congress, this Anjuman expresses its sympathy with the Association.

33. *Anjuman Islamia, Umballa, Punjab.*—A majority of the members of this Anjuman expressed their agreement with the United Indian Patriotic Association, the remainder saying they would like to see the pamphlets issued by that Association before giving an opinion.

34. *Anjuman Islamia, Jullundur, Punjab.*—A telegram was received on October 1st from the Secretary of this Anjuman, stating that the Anjuman agreed with the United Indian Patriotic Association.

35. *Anjuman-i-Mufidul Islam, Jingapara, Mohanganj, Mymensing, Bengal.*—On September 29th a meeting of this Anjuman was held, at which it was decided that the Anjuman was entirely opposed to the National Congress.

36. *National Muhammadan Association, Branch Pubna, Bengal.*—The Secretary of this Association states that the Association sympathises with the United Indian Patriotic Association, and adds :—" The members of the Association observe that the so-called National Congress is not a Congress held at the united desire of the different sects or races. It is an assemblage of certain ambitious Hindus— the Bengalis taking the warmest interest in it. Their aim is hostile to the administration of the Government as such, and as the Bengalis entertain bitter feelings against the Musalmans, and do not like that the Muhammadans should

ever prosper, it is not desirable that any Musalman should join the Congress."

37. *Anjuman Islamia, Ajmere, Rajputana.*—A meeting of this Anjuman was held on October 7th, in the Dargah of Moin-ud-din Chisti, the famous dervish. Kazi Syed Imam-ud-din, a descendant of the great saint, presided. It is stated that at this meeting nearly 4,000 Muhammadans were present. It was decided that the meeting was entirely opposed to the National Congress, and that the Anjuman should be regarded as a branch of the United Indian Patriotic Association.

38. *Muhammadan Central National Association, Punjab, Lahore.*—A meeting of this Association was held on October 7th, at which it was decided that the Association was opposed to the National Congress, and sympathised with the United Indian Patriotic Association.

39. *Bilgram Institute, Bilgram, Hardvi, Oudh.*—A meeting of this Institute was held on September 30th, at which the following resolutions were passed :—

(1). That this Institute, composed of Hindus and Muhammadans, is wholly opposed to the Congress, and has not the least sympathy with it.

(2). That anyone favouring the cause of the Congress will be considered as no longer fit to continue as a member of this Institute.

40. *Anjuman-i-Islamia, Rangpur, Bengal.*—A letter was received from the Secretary of this Anjuman, stating that the Anjuman strongly disapproved of the National Congress.

41. *Anjuman-i-Tahzib-i-Islam, Arrah, Bengal.*—A meeting of this Anjuman was held on October 16th in the Imperial Jumma Musjid. Haji Abdul Hakim, Hakim Mahomed Yasin and Mirza Mahomed Ismail, *B.A.*, *B.L.*, spoke against the Congress, after which resolutions were passed condemning the Congress and approving of the United Indian Patriotic Association.

42. *Anjuman-i-Ahbab, Bombay.*—In reply to a letter of the Secretary of the United Indian Patriotic Association, the Secretary of this Anjuman, Khan Bahadur Gholam Mahomed Munshi, wrote to say that a meeting of this Anjuman was held on August 4th, to oppose the National Congress. This meeting was convened by Shamsul Ulama Kazi Sharif Abdul Latif; Mirza Hosain Khan, Solicitor; Mahomed Hosain Hakim, Barrister; Esa Ben Khalifa, and the Secretary of the Anjuman. A very large number of Muhammadans of Bombay were present.

43. *Anjuman Islamia, Peshawar, Punjab.*—A meeting of this Anjuman was held on October 14th : the Congress agitator, Mr. Bhimji, was also present. The following Sirdars of Pathan tribes were present :—Kazi Abdul Kadir, President ; Kazi Syed Ahmed Khan, *C.I.E.*, Vice-President ; Kazi Tila Mahomed Khan, Secretary ; Jelal-ud-din Khan, Under-Secretary ; Arbab Mahomed Hosain Khan ; Khan Bahadur Ibrahim Khan, Yusafzai ; Arbab Farid Khan ; Arbab Fateh Khan ; Arbab Mahomed Khan of Sumla ; Kazi Abdul Wahid, Manager of Budruddin and Co. ; Haji Arbab Gholam Hyder Khan ; Kazi Amin Jan ; Kazi Agha Jan ; Kazi Moghal Jan ; Haji Mahomed Khan ; Syed Mir Ahmed Shah, &c., &c.

After several speeches—Mr. Bhimji also being allowed to have his say—the following resolutions were passed :—

(1). That this Muhammadan meeting has no kind of sympathy or agreement with these people who are travelling about lecturing in favour of the National Congress.

(2). That this meeting offers its thanks to those Anjumans of Calcutta, Bombay, Madras, the North-West Provinces and the Punjab, which have at a most expedient time warned Muhammadans against the misfortunes that would befall them from joining the Congress ; and that this meeting agrees with the opinions of those Anjumans.

(3). That if any Muhammadan of Peshawar be induced by deceitful methods to join the Congress, and thereby bring dishonour on the Muhammadan nation, he must be understood to be in no sense a representative of the Muhammadans of Peshawar, but must be regarded as one who has exiled himself from the pale of Islam.

44. *Anjuman Islamia, Lucknow, Oudh.*—This Anjuman is opposed to the National Congress. On October 14th a meeting was held, at which it was resolved that the Secretary of the United Indian Patriotic Association be informed in writing that the Anjuman agrees with the objects of the United Indian Patriotic Association, and has great pleasure in joining it.

45. *Anjuman-i-Movey-i-dul Islam, Saharanpur, North-Western Provinces.*—This Anjuman held a meeting on October 26th, at which the following Rule was added to the Rules of the Anjuman :—

"That this Anjuman, after full consideration, is opposed to the National Congress, which it regards as prejudicial to the interests of the whole people of India, and extremely prejudicial for Muhammadans."

46. *Sind Branch Central National Muhammadan Association, Karachi, Sind.*—A general meeting of this Association was held at Karachi on October 28th, after consultation with the several sub-branches in the Province. Several speeches were made, of which the leading one was from Khan Bahadur Hasan Ali Effendi, President of the Association. The following resolutions were passed :—

(1). That the Central National Muhammadan Association, Sind Branch, considers the aims and objects of the Indian National Congress, if carried out, will vitally injure Muhammadan interests.

(2). That the Association is strongly opposed to the Congress.

(3). That the Association sympathises with the aims of the United Indian Patriotic Association.

47. *Anjuman Hami-i-Islam, Nagpur, Central Provinces.*—The inaugural meeting of this Anjuman was held on October 28th in the Sadar Bazar, old mosque, two hundred people being present. The following resolutions were passed :—

(1). That this Anjuman, after full consideration and discussion of the aims and objects of the so-called National Congress, is of opinion that the movements of the Congress are revolutionary and prejudicial to the Moslem community ; that the voice of the Congress is not the voice of the *Nation ;* that its demands are premature, and the grievances which it alleges, imaginary. This meeting therefore protests against all its movements, and refuses to co-operate with it in any of its undertakings.

(Carried with one dissentient voice, that of a self-elected delegate to the Madras Congress).

(2). That this Anjuman has held its inaugural meeting to-day with two objects—(1) for the glory of freedom of India in a general way ; and (2) for the welfare and prosperity of the Muhammadan community in particular ; and with a view to give full effect to these resolutions, earnestly recommends that this Anjuman, without further delay, should incorporate itself with, and record its cordial sympathy with the objects and deliberations of the United Indian Patriotic Association.

(Carried unanimously).

(3). That this Anjuman affirms that should any Muhammadan of Nagpur join or associate himself in any way with any Congress meetings to be held at Nagpur, or allow himself to be appointed as a delegate to the Allahabad Congress, he will be considered as representing himself alone, and as a renegade from the Moslem community.

(Carried unanimously).

(4). That a copy of the resolutions passed by this Anjuman be communicated to the Anjuman Nasar-ul-Islam, and other similar Anjumans in each province, and that those Anjumans be requested, with the help of similar bodies, to adopt such measures as they consider best calculated to give effect to these resolutions.

(Carried unanimously).

(5). That this Anjuman does humbly offer its dutiful and loyal gratitude to Her Most Gracious Majesty the Queen-Empress for her benign Government, and heartily wishes her a long life, and happy reign over the great British Empire.

(Carried unanimously).

48. *Hugli District National Muhammadan Association, Bengal.*—The following letter, dated November 14th, has been received from the Secretary of this Association by the Hon'ble Secretary of the United Indian Patriotic Association :—

(1). "With reference to your Urdu circular and subsequent correspondences, I have the honour to inform you that the Hugli District National Muhammadan Association has at last agreed to join with the expressions of its Parent Association in showing every sympathy with the objects of the United Indian Patriotic Association.

(2). "I have further to state that the Hindu members of this Association do not agree with their Moslem brethren in para. 1 of this letter."

49. *Anjuman Umumeiya Islamia, Dinapore, Bengal.*— On August 21st a meeting of this Anjuman was held, at which about 1,200 people were present. All present, both those who were members of the Anjuman and those who were not, unanimously agreed with the objects of the United Indian Patriotic Association. They all cried out in Arabic—*Iqtadaito bihazal Imam :* ("We will follow it as we do our priest in the mosque at prayers").

50. *Anjuman Islamia, Gurdaspur, Punjab.*—The Hindus held a National Congress meeting at Gurdaspur on the occasion of the visit of Mr. Bhimji, and appointed two Muhammadans—Nabi Baksh and Ali Mahomed—as delegates; the latter is not a Punjabi, but an inhabitant of Burmah. The Muhammadans of Gurdaspur then called a general meeting of this Anjuman on November 4th, at which Nabi Baksh was also present. The Secretary of the Anjuman, Mahomed Shams-ud-din, then asked all present if the Muhammadans of Gurdaspur had appointed Nabi Baksh as their delegate. They all cried out—" No ; we have no sympathy with the Congress." The President then asked Nabi Baksh why, when no Muhammadan of Gurdaspur had appointed him as a delegate, he was going to join the Congress as their representative. He replied that he went to represent himself alone, and did not call himself a delegate of the Muhammadans ; but as the condition of the Muhammadans had gone from bad to worse, and the Muhammadans did not follow the laws of the Prophet, and were Musalmans only in name, he had no trust in Muhammadans, who called the National Congress a bad thing. Other people then made speeches, and one speaker said to Nabi Baksh that if the condition of the Muhammadans was bad, he ought to try to help them, and when he would render no assistance at such a time, he must be regarded as a renegade from Islam. The following resolution was then passed :—

" That the Anjuman Islamia of Gurdaspur has no kind of sympathy with the objects of the National Congress, and that Sheikh Nabi Baksh and Ali Mahomed are the representatives of no Muhammadans, but are self-constituted delegates, and that a copy of the proceedings be sent to the Secretary of the United Indian Patriotic Association."

51. *Anjuman Islamia, Vizagapatam, Madras.*—A meeting of this Anjuman was held on October 28th, at

which it was agreed that all members of the Anjuman were against the National Congress, and sympathised with the United Indian Patriotic Association.

52. *Anjuman Islamia, Roorkee, North-Western Provinces.*—A meeting of this Anjuman was held in the evening of November 17th, at Piran Kaliar, four miles out of Roorkee, at the tomb of the great Saint Ala-ud-din Sabir. It is said that nearly 15,000 people were present. The President of this meeting was Iltifat Ahmed, the great Dervish of Radauli. It was decided that the Muhammadans should have nothing to do with the National Congress, and should carry their opposition to it to the utmost possible extreme.

53. *Anjuman Nasir-ul-Islam, Nagpur, Central Provinces.*—The members of this Anjuman and of the Anjuman Islamia, Nagpur, held a united meeting at which 500 persons were present. In this meeting some Congress-wallas were present. After many speeches the following resolution was passed by a majority of votes :—

" That the Association is opposed to the Congress, and if any Musalman of Nagpur should join the Congress, he should not be regarded as a delegate of the Muhammadans, but should be considered his own delegate."

PUBLIC MEETINGS OF HINDUS AND MUHAMMADANS
HELD TO CONDEMN
THE NATIONAL CONGRESS.

A SHORT account of some of the public meetings that have been held in different parts of India is here given. The list is far from complete. Many meetings took place before any attempt was made to keep a record. And many meetings have probably since been held, accounts of which have escaped our observation. But the list, it is believed, contains an account of the most important meetings, and is sufficient to show that, even in the small fraction of the community which in India takes any interest in political matters, opinion is by no means so unanimous in favour of the proposals of the National Congress as its supporters affirm.—ED.

MEETING AT ALLAHABAD, N.-W. P., FEBRUARY 27TH, 1888.

A VERY large meeting was held at Allahabad against the National Congress. Three thousand Muhammadans—Sunnis and Shias—were present. Hafiz Maulvi Mahomed Husain, who is a very highly respected priest, and who belongs to the very old and celebrated family of the Saint Shah Hujjat-ul-lah, was the President of this meeting. The President, Fazl-ul-lah, *B.A.*, Mahomed Azim-ud-din, Mobarik Hosain, Syed Zakir Hosain, Syed Mahdi Hosain, Shaukat Ali, Syed Mahomed Nuh, Shaikh Akbar Hosain, Abdul Ghafar, Abdur Razzak, Mazhar Hosain, and Maulvi Mahomed Ibrahim, made speeches against the National Congress. It was unanimously agreed that the proposals of the National Congress would bring misfortunes to the country at large, and especially to Muhammadans, and that the Muhammadans have no sympathy with the National Congress, and should have none.

MEETING AT LUCKNOW, MAY 6TH, 1888.

ON May 6th, an enormous open-air mass-meeting of Muhammadans was held in the Kaisar Bagh at Lucknow. Munshi Imtiaz Ali presided. The shop-keepers shut their shops and the Muhammadan carriage-drivers drove people to the meeting free of charge. It is estimated that the attendance was 20,000. The meeting condemned the National Congress in the strongest terms. The meeting was divided into five sections, and addressed simultaneously by five speakers. No such Muhammadan meeting on politics has ever been known in India. At the close of the speeches the whole assembly united in the afternoon prayers, enjoined by the Muhammadan religion.

MEETING AT BARAON, ZILA ALLAHABAD, N.-W. P., JULY 19TH, 1888.

THE President of this meeting was Babu Mahabir Narain Singh, Talukdar of Baraon. Two thousand people were present, including many zemindars and influential men. The President, Bhairo Singh Varma, Pandit Ram Dat Singh, and Syed Madad Ali, Khan Bahadur, made speeches against the proposals of the National Congress, and the following resolutions were unanimously passed :—

(1). That this meeting does not sympathise with the National Congress.

(2). Inasmuch as the supporters of the Congress are travelling about in various places deceiving the people, that this meeting should appoint some people who should visit different places and point out the evils of the National Congress, because if any civil war take place, no trace of the Bengalis will be found, and the whole brunt of the misfortune will fall on Hindu Rajputs and Muhammadan Pathans.

Babu Mahabir Pershad said he would defray all the expenses incurred in this work from his own pocket.

MEETING AT BENARES, N.-W. P., JULY 23RD, 1888.

HIS HIGHNESS THE MAHARAJA OF BENARES, *G.C.S.I.*, called this meeting in the Town Hall. Two hundred and fifty influential men and great Pandits of Benares were present. Raja Shiva Pershad read a lecture by the Maharaja, which, on account of weakness, he was unable to read himself.

MEETING AT BENARES, N.-W. P., JULY 28TH, 1888.

THE learned Pandits of Benares summoned this meeting. Pandit Raja Ram Shastri, a celebrated scholar, and Pandit Chunaman Rao Dhar, made speeches against the National Congress, and criticised its aims and its writings, and said that there was no necessity for the Congress agitation, and proved from the Puranas, the sacred books of the Hindus, that the agitation was most unjustifiable.

MEETING AT BOMBAY, AUGUST 4TH, 1888.

A LARGE meeting of Muhammadans was held at Bombay on this date, presided over by His Highness Agha Akbar Shah, and including respectable members of all the sections of the Muhammadan community at Bombay. The Kazi of the city, Shamsul Ulama Kazi Abdul Latif, was present. The meeting decided that the Muhammadans of Bombay should hold aloof from the Congress. This meeting was extremely important, inasmuch as the President of the last National Congress was a Muhammadan of Bombay, and it was popularly supposed that the Bombay Muhammadans sympathised with the movement. Subsequently a small meeting of the Anjuman Islamia was held, at which about 20 persons were present, which decided to send delegates to the next National Congress.

MEETING AT KARCHANA, ALLAHABAD, N.-W. P., AUGUST 6TH, 1888.

THIS meeting was held at the house of Babu Beni Pershad Singh, Talukdar. More than 1,000 people belonging to both nations—Hindus and Muhammadans—were present. Many speeches were made, and finally it was resolved that the meeting was opposed to the National Congress, and would exercise as strenuous an opposition to it as possible.

MEETING AT BARAON, ZILA ALLAHABAD, N.-W. P., AUGUST 12TH, 1888.

THE President of this meeting was Babu Mahabir Narain Singh.

The President, Thakur Bhairo Singh, Thakur Shiva Pershad, Thakur Barja Baksh Singh, and Thakur Raghunath Narain Singh, made speeches against the National Congress. A permanent Anti-Congress Committee was formed, consisting of many Hindus and Muhammadans with Patrons, President, and Vice-Presidents as given below :—

Patrons :

Raja Bhivanda Singh, Bahadur, Raja of Bijepur.

Raja Partab Singh, Bahadur, Raja of Mandha.

Raja Banspat Singh, Bahadur, Raja of Kishengarh.

President :

Babu Mahabir Pershad Narain Singh.

Vice-Presidents :

Koer Ram Singh, Bahadur.

Lal Chatterpatti Singh.

Maulvi Abdul Aziz.

MEETING AT MAINPURI, N.-W. P., AUGUST 14TH, 1888.

ON this day a large Anti-Congress meeting, consisting of the leading gentlemen of the town, mostly Rajputs and Muhammadans, was held at Mainpuri.   Maharaja Ram Partab Singh, Bahadur, Raja of Mainpuri, presided.   After a short speech by the Chairman, the Hon'ble Sir Syed Ahmed's speech delivered at Meerut was read and heard with cheers, and the following resolutions were passed :—

(1).   The meeting has no sympathy with the Congress.

(2).   The gentlemen who presented themselves at the Madras Congress were not delegates of the people.

MEETING AT GORAKHPUR, N.-W. P., AUGUST 21ST, 1888.

ON this day a meeting was held in the Mission High School, Gorakhpur.   His Highness Maharaja Koomar Lal Khadja Bahadur of Majhowli, presided.   Rao Chintaman and Rao Bal Krishna addressed the meeting, and the following resolution was passed :—

" That we should not associate with the Congress."

MEETING AT SHAHJEHANPUR, N.-W. P., AUGUST
30TH, 1888.

A GREAT meeting of Muhammadans was held on this date at Shahjehanpur.   All men of influence and Pathans of every clan inhabiting the country were present.   Ahmed Hasan Khan was President.   Maulvi Mahomed Ismail, Mahomed Habib-ul-lah Khan, and Munshi Dost Mahomed Khan made speeches, and showed that the proposals of the Congress were not only prejudicial to the Muhammadans, but were dangerous for the country at large.   The following resolutions were passed :—

(1).   That the Muhammadans of Shahjehanpur regard the objects of the National Congress as a deadly poison for their community, and that therefore they neither have now nor will have in future any kind of sympathy with the Congress.

(2). That no person should attend the approaching Congress at Allahabad as a delegate of the Muhammadans of Shahjehanpur, and if any person should pretend to do so, he should be regarded as the delegate of himself alone, and as having no connection with the Muhammadans of Shahjehanpur.

MEETING AT LUCKNOW, SEPTEMBER, 2ND, 1888.

THE Princes of Lucknow belonging to the old Royal Family of Oudh, and all the men of high position, were present at this meeting. Among those present were the following:—Nawab Mirza Mahdi Ali, Khan Bahadur; Prince Mirza Mahomed Taqi, Khan Bahadur, nephew of the late King of Oudh; Prince Mirza Masud Qadr of the old Royal House of Delhi; Nawab Faghfur Mirza, Bahadur; Nawab Saif-ud-Daulah, Bahadur; Nawab Mahomed Jafir Ali, Khan Bahadur; Nawab Shah Mirza, Bahadur; Nawab Mahomed Baqr Ali, Khan Bahadur; Nawab Sultan Bakht, Bahadur; Mirza Agha Ali, Khan Bahadur; Munshi Mahomed Imtiaz Ali, Rai Bahadur; Pandit Sri Kishen; Munshi Newal Kishore, *C. I. E.*, and others.

This meeting was held at the house of Nawab Mirza Mahdi Ali, who was President. After several speeches the following resolution was unanimously passed:—

"That this meeting refuses to send delegates to any meeting of the National Congress, and that any one claiming to represent the higher and middle classes of the native community of Lucknow at any meeting of the Congress, must be taken to represent himself alone."

MEETING AT LUDHIANA, PUNJAB, SEPTEMBER 22ND, 1888.

A MUHAMMADAN Anti-Congress meeting was held on this day at Ludhiana, to record total disapproval of the National Congress.

MEETING AT BASTI, N.-W. P., SEPTEMBER 23RD, 1888.

A MEETING was held on this date at Basti. Basti is a small zila (district), but 200 people were present. Maulvi Abdus Sami made a speech against the National Congress. The following resolutions were passed :—

(1). That this meeting is entirely opposed to the National Congress.

(2). That this meeting should send no delegates to the National Congress.

MEETING OF THE CHIEF PRIESTS OF DELHI,
SEPTEMBER 23RD, 1888.

A GREAT meeting of all the Maulvis of Delhi, of all sects of Muhammadans—Sunni, Shiah, Hanafi, and Ahl-i-Hadis (formerly known as Wahabis)—took place on this date in the Fatehpuri mosque. Five thousand Muhammadans were present. Prince Suleiman Shah, of the family of the old Emperors of India, was in the chair. Maulvi Nazir Hosain, a man of enormous influence throughout the whole of India, the head of the Ahl-i-Hadis, and one of the most learned men alive in India, was present. Maulvi Abdul Haq, a very celebrated Maulvi of the Hanafi sect, was also present and made a speech, in which he opposed the National Congress, and said that it was extremely harmful for Muhammadans. He proposed the following resolution :—

" That the Muhammadans of Delhi are entirely opposed to the proposals of the Congress."

Maulvi Nazir Hosain seconded this resolution, and afterwards offered up a prayer to God to preserve the Muhammadans from the evil effects of this Congress.

Hafiz Aziz-ud-din then made a speech and proposed the following resolution :—

" That the Muhammadans of Delhi are fully loyal to the English Government."

Hakim Gholam Raja Khan seconded this, and it was carried.

MEETING AT MUTTRA, N.-W. P., SEPTEMBER 24TH, 1888.

A MEETING was held here to-day in the Municipal Hall, at which about one thousand Muhammadans and Hindus were present. Maulvi Syed Farid-ud-din Shah, Raïs of Agra, and Mahomed Abdul Hadi, Pleader and Municipal Commissioner, addressed the assembly at some length denouncing the National Congress, and a resolution was passed declaring that those present at the meeting should have nothing to do with that movement.

MEETING AT DELHI, OCTOBER 5TH, 1888.

A VERY important meeting of the Muhammadans against the National Congress was held in the Town Hall. About 2,000 Muhammadans were present. Prince Mirza Suleiman Shah, of the family of the Moghal Emperors, was President. The following gentlemen were present :—Prince Mahomed Iqbal Shah, Nawab Bashir-ud-din Ahmed Khan, Khan Bahadur Hadi Hosain Khan, Khan Bahadur Mahomed Nizam-ud-din Khan, Mahomed Inayetur Rahman, Nawab Mahomed Ibrahim Ali Khan, Nawab Sharf-ud-din Ahmed Khan, Mahomed Ikram-ul-lah Khan, Bhaya Shamshere Bahadur, Haji Syed Mahomed, Imam of the Imperial Mosque of Delhi, Shamsul Ulama Khan Bahadur, Munshi Zaka-ul-lah, Munshi Nazir Ahmed, Maulvi Karim Bakhsh, Syed Sultan Mirza, Hafiz Aziz-ud-din, Maulvi Inayet Ahmed, Nawab Ahmed Ali Khan, Nawab Shuja-ud-din Ahmed Khan, Hakim Mahomed Gholam Raza Khan, Hakim Mahomed Wasil Khan, Shaikh Hafiz-ul-lah, Maulvi Altaf Hosain (a famous poet), Shahzada Mirza Mahomed Ashraf, and others.

Maulvi Nazir Ahmed delivered a very effective lecture against the Congress, and pointed out the bad results that would follow from it for the Muhammadans and for the country. The following resolutions were then passed :—

(1). Proposed by Mahomed Ikram-ul-lah Khan and seconded by Munshi Zaka-ul-lah, late Professor at the Muir College, Allahabad—" That inasmuch as the objects of the National Congress are harmful to the country generally, and to the Muhammadans in particular, this meeting has no sympathy with the Congress."

(2). Proposed by Mahomed Inayetur Rahman Khan and seconded by Hakim Gholam Raza Khan—" That because the well-wishers of our nation and of the country have, after full consideration, established the United Indian Patriotic Association, this meeting expresses its full sympathy with the objects of that Association."

(3). Proposed by Hafiz Aziz-ud-din and seconded by Shaikh Hafiz-ul-lah—" That for the reasons mentioned in resolution (2) a branch of the United Indian Patriotic Association be established in Delhi."

(4). Proposed by Shahzada Mirza Mahomed Ashraf and seconded by Khan Bahadur Mahomed Nizam-ud-din— " That if any Muhammadans of Delhi join the National Congress, they should be regarded as representing themselves alone, and should not be considered as delegates or representatives of the Muhammadans of Delhi."

MEETING AT SAHARANPUR, N.-W. P., OCTOBER 5TH, 1888.

A MEETING was held in the big mosque after the Friday prayers, and about 5,000 people were present. Maulvi Abdul Ghani and Hafiz Fakr-ud-din, Imam of the mosque, pointed out the evils of the National Congress before the commencement of prayers. The 5,000 Muhammadans who were present agreed that they were opposed to the National Congress, and that no one ought to sympathise with it.

MEETING AT JAUNPUR, N.-W. P., OCTOBER 6TH, 1888.

AT an influential and well-attended meeting held on the evening of October 6th, Raja Hari Har Dat Dube, Bahadur, of Jaunpur, delivered a lecture against the National Congress, which, he said, had greatly increased the enmity between the Hindus and Muhammadans, and with regard to which the Government should take early steps with a view to stop such agitations. There were present :—Maulvi Abdul Majid, Barrister-at-Law ; Maulvi Mahomed Ibrahim Khan, Bahadur ; Maulvis Mahomed Jan, Basit Ali and Kazi Mahomed Khalil, Honorary Magistrates ; Raja Shankar Dat, Bahadur ; Maulvi Mahomed Syed Khan, Raïs ; Maulvi Syed Mahomed of Kheta-Sarai ; Mufties Zainulabdin, Hyder Hosain and Ata Hosain of Mufti-mohalla ; Dr. Sastewar Roy ; Babus Charu Chandar, Damodar Das, and Parsotan Das ; Syed Zahid Hosain and Kazi Azizuddin Ahmed, Deputy Collectors ; Syed Habib-ul-lah, C. S. ; Pandit Shankar Lal, Tehsildar, and many other respectable Raïses, Vakils, and Zemindars.

A branch of the United Patriotic Association was formed, and the following Raïses accepted membership :— Raja Hari Har Dube, Bahadur, President ; Raja Shankar Dat ; Maulvi Mahomed Ibrahim Khan, Bahadur ; Maulvi Mahomed Syed Khan ; Maulvi Mobarak Hosain ; Maulvi Basit Ali ; Maulvi Mahomed Jamil ; Mufties Zainulabdin, Hyder Hosain and Ata Hosain ; Maulvi Mahomed Hanif ; Maulvi Farid-ul-Haq ; Syed Ali Hosain ; Babu Damodar Das ; Maulvi Mahomed Ali of Machhlishahr ; Maulvi Mahomed Salem and other gentlemen with Maulvi Syed Mahmud, a very intelligent Pleader, as Secretary.

Maulvi Syed Kaim Ali, Raïs of Kheta-Sarai, offered a donation of Rs. 50 towards the Association.

After the above proceedings the following resolution was passed :—

(1). The Hindus and Muhammadans of Jaunpur shall not send any delegate to the Allahabad meeting of the Congress. If any one goes there he will not be our representative. (Proposed by Raja Hari Har Dat, Bahadur, and seconded by Mufti Hyder Hosain).

Maulvi Abdul Majid then thanked the Raja for the good lecture he delivered and for the courage he showed in denouncing the Congress so candidly. Three hundred copies of a pamphlet by Maulvi Ahmed-ul-lah, Government pensioner, and several copies of a poem by Mr. Safdar Hosain against the National Congress, were distributed to those present.

MEETING AT ETAWAH, N.-W. P., ON NOVEMBER 2ND, 1888.

A MEETING of the Anti-National Congress party was held here on 2nd November, 1888, in the Imambara of Nawab Mehdi Ali, who was President. Haji Mumtaz Ali Khan, Honorary Magistrate, and all the Muhammadan gentlemen of Etawah, were present. Several speeches were made, and the following resolutions were unanimously passed :— " First, that the Muhammadans of Etawah are entirely opposed to the objects of the National Congress ; and second, that they sympathise with the aims of the United Indian Patriotic Association."

MEETING AT DACCA, NOVEMBER 11TH, 1888.

AN open-air meeting of Muhammadans was held at Dacca at 3 P. M., on the above-mentioned date. It was attended by about 2,000 persons. All the gentry of the city were present. Delegates came from Mymensingh and other districts. Several letters of sympathy were received from the districts of Eastern Bengal. Munshi Gholam Mustafa, one of the leading gentlemen of the city, whose name the other party had used without his authority as a staunch supporter of the Congress, presided, and declared that he had no connection with the Congress, and that his name had been used against his will. The following resolutions were unanimously passed with much enthusiasm :—

(1). That no Indian should join the Congress.

(2). That no Muhammadan should join the Congress.

(3). That the Muhammadans named by the Hindus as their delegates are not the delegates of the Dacca Muhammadans. The Dacca Muhammadans have not elected them, and have no connection with them.

MEETING AT LUCKNOW, NOVEMBER 22ND, 1888.

A GREAT meeting of the aristocracy of Oudh was held at Lucknow on November 23nd, having been convened by the British Indian Association of the Oudh Talukdars. It was decided to form a new Anti-Congress Association, named the *Indian Loyal Association*, with His Highness the Maharaja of Benares as Patron of the new Association and the Hon'ble Maharaja Partab Narain Singh as President. A resolution was also carried condemning the Congress, and saying that if any Hindu or Muhammadan of these Provinces should attend the National Congress, he should not be considered as a delegate from these Provinces. Many very influential men, Hindu and Muhammadan, were present.

www.ingramcontent.com/pod-product-compliance
Lightning Source LLC
Chambersburg PA
CBHW030848270326
41928CB00007B/1270